Joanne Veselak

Treasury of

Teaching Activities for

Elementary Language Arts

Treasury of

Teaching Activities for

Elementary Language Arts

RICHARD A. THOMPSON

Parker Publishing Company, Inc.

West Nyack, New York

Library of Congress Cataloging in Publication Data

Thompson, Richard A
   Treasury of teaching activities for elementary
language arts.

   1. Language arts (Elementary) 2. Creative
activities and seat work. I. Title.
LB1575.8.T48   372.6'044   74-28172
ISBN 0-13-930446-0

Printed in the United States of America

A Word About the Value of
This Book to the Teacher

This book will help you provide a rich, substantive language arts program for your students. All teachers search for imaginative techniques that deal with communication skills, and this book of teaching activities will, indeed, be a "treasury" of tested, practical ways you can use to help your students *communicate* effectively.

It will help save you hours of labor dreaming up instructional activities, and you'll note that every language arts area is covered. Every chapter is chock-full of successful activities to help you individualize and improve your instruction. Also, note the format. Each activity is presented with title, purpose, materials, procedures, and illustrations wherever appropriate. You will not have to hunt around for information when making use of an idea. The organization is built on the basis of convenience to the user.

Frequently we fail to teach a skill because we haven't provided sufficient instructional dosage. Having presented information once or twice, we tend to move on to something else. Using your bank of successful teaching ideas, you will be able quickly to prescribe appropriate instruction to meet your students' learning needs with highly motivating activities. Then too, you will be able to present independent learning experiences for certain students while providing corrective instruction for those in need. Providing you with such versatility is a major value of this book.

Armed with these proven teaching strategies, you will have the essential material you need for interesting language arts programs. Creative teaching ideas, as you know from experience when using your own, tend to electrify the learning environment. Students do get excited when interested, and are hesitant to stop. Perhaps this is a problem in using creative activities of this type, but it is this student interest that makes you an exciting teacher.

Each chapter is related to a particular language art skill. For example, Chapter 1 contains games and unique ideas for spelling. Is there any other area that needs student motivation more? Independent and group spelling activities are found in Chapter 2. Each language art topic has been covered and organized into games and independent and group activities, providing you with flexibility in your intraclass grouping arrangements.

Grade level designations have been abandoned in this book, and the reason is this: these teaching ideas are pertinent whenever there is need to teach a particular skill. At every grade level, students will have a wide range of achievement levels. Use these activities whenever you need them, since grade level designations are too often misleading and restrictive.

With the exception of brief chapter introductions, the activities will do the talking in this book, and I believe what they have to say will help you to greatly enrich your Language Arts program.

Richard A. Thompson

ACKNOWLEDGMENTS

Every manuscript receives care and creative input from several people. As the author of this book, I would like to acknowledge the helpful efforts of the many people who have contributed their talented ideas and energies to making it. First, there were the editors and reviewers who deserve my thanks for their perceptive suggestions. Also, there were many fine activities presented to me by my teaching friends who merit a note of thanks. Each of you, whether a teaching colleague or a reciprocal in a teacher-student relationship, has made a significant contribution to this book. I gratefully appreciate your input.* It is my wife, Janet, who should be given more than a word of thanks because she worked and contributed as much as anyone, including myself. As a token of my appreciation, I proclaim her co-author. And lastly, to Kim, David, Tim, and Carol; I say thanks to each of you for providing me with sustaining motivation.

R.A.T.

*When the drawings got tough, I relied on my artist friend, Joe Harkiewicz, who has my thanks.

Contents

Treasury of

Teaching Activities for

Elementary Language Arts

CHAPTER 1

24 Oxygenic Gaming Activities for Effective Spelling Programs

Unquestionably, a most important function of a teacher is motivation. Coaches give pep talks inducing pride in their players, urging wherewithal performances, praising and coercing. Excellent teachers are above all good coaches because they realize that learning takes place only following motivation and learning is sustained only with continuous motivation.

Spelling is a subject that seems to require exceptional adeptness on the part of the teacher to keep students vigorously interested. With the typical spelling program running like this:

> Monday—words are introduced
> Tuesday—words are written in context
> Wednesday—skill exercise
> Thursday—trial test
> Friday—test,

is it any wonder students are apt to find spelling a boring rut? It takes acumen and creativity on the teacher's part to break the stifling routine euphemistically called a spelling program.

Chapters 1 and 2 are your spelling treasure chests. It is in this chapter that you have available gaming activities in sufficient quantity to keep your spelling program viable and interesting all year long. Because games are intrinsically motivating, they provide that essential function of yours as soon as you tell your students they are going to play a game.

Most teachers use a textbook as the core of their spelling curriculum.

Whether you use a spelling text or have devised your own program, you will find these games useful addenda stimulating your students to higher plateaus of achievement.

Begin enriching your program by using one or two of these games per week. You will notice changing attitudes toward spelling immediately as you run your rutless spelling program.

Title:	**"Clue Me In"**
Purpose:	To provide spelling drill.
Activity:	Game.
Materials:	Cards with one spelling word on each.
Procedure:	Cards are placed face down. Alternately, students select a card without looking at the word on it. The card is held or displayed so the class can see the word.
	Seated students raise their hands and give their team member one-word clues as he tries to guess the mystery word. He can call on only three students for clues. If the word is not identified, he then puts the card back in the stack and the other team has a turn. For each word identified one point is given.

Title:	**"Roots and Affixes"**
Purpose:	To teach students that the meaning of words is changed by the addition of prefixes and suffixes.
Activity:	Game.
Materials:	A list of prefixes, suffixes, and root words.
Procedure:	Give the list to each student. Tell them to see how many new words they can form. Set a time limit. Students may also work in teams.

Example:　　Root word—like　　　　　　　order

liked	orders
likes	ordered
likely	orderly
likeness	orderliness
likeable	orderable
likeableness	disorder
likelihood	disordered
liken	disorderable
likewise	disorderly
unlike	disorderliness
unlikely	unordered
dislike	
dislikeable	
dislikeness	
disliking	
disliken	

Title:	**"Spelling Card Game"**
Purpose:	To help students correctly spell words.
Activity:	Game.
Materials:	About four sets of the letters of the alphabet made on sturdy cards and a score sheet.
Procedure:	Place all cards face down on the table with each player drawing six cards. Whoever is first tries to spell a word with the letters he has. If he cannot, then he can put not more than three of his letters back and draw three more. A point is scored for each letter used.

Title: **"Spelling Race"**

Purpose: To provide practice in visually discriminating spelling words.

Activity: Game.

Procedure: On two chalkboards or charts draw a race track as illustrated. Place scrambled spelling words from "start" to "finish" as illustrated. Use all of the spelling list on each board, but vary the order.

Divide students into two teams. A member from each team goes to each board to unscramble the first word. As quickly as possible, he gives chalk to the next person on his team to unscramble the second word. If a student does not know the word, he can ask for clues from his team. One word clues can be given, but only two clues can be given for each word. The next student tries the same word. Example: *rief* Clue #1: "hot" Clue #2: "smoke"

The team that unscrambles all the words and reaches the finish line first wins the race. If the seated students call out a spelling word, a point is deducted from their score.

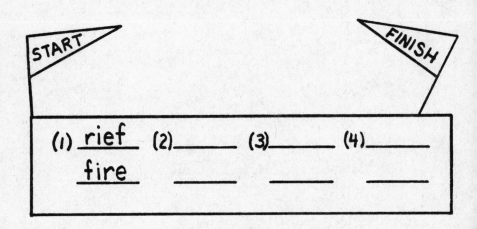

Title: **"Computer Spelling"**

Purpose: To give students practice in applying spelling rules for the pluralization of words or in adding suffixes

Activity   Game.

Materials: Decorate with construction paper a medium-sized cardboard box with one side painted to look like a computer.
Cut a slot in the side of the box. You will also need some
cards to simulate computer cards. Make a list of words
and write a word on each card using two colors with half
the words in one color and the other half in another color.

Procedure: Have the box placed on a table, and the bottom side
facing the class. Tell the class they are going to play
computer spelling. Explain to them that there will be two
teams, and each will take turns in sending up a team
member. Each team will have its own color of words
written on computer cards. The cards are placed face
down in two stacks. The student draws a card from his
team's stack, and attempts to put the word in its plural
form. If he is successful, he feeds the card into the computer through the slot. The game is finished when each
team has used all its cards. By totaling the number of
cards in each color, the class can tell which team won.

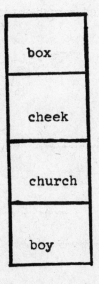

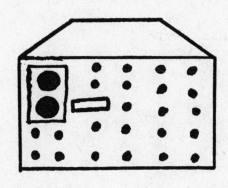

Title: **"Homonym Concentration"**

Purpose: To provide drill on homonyms.

Activity: Game.

Materials: Ten to 20 pairs of homonyms are placed on cards.

Procedure: This game is played like the game of CONCENTRA-
                   TION. Shuffle the cards and place them face down. Each
                   player turns over two cards, endeavoring to match the
                   two homonyms. If the cards do not match, they are
                   turned face down again, and the next player has a turn. If
                   a player makes a match, he is allowed another turn. The
                   winner is the one with the most pairs. (This game can be
                   played using synonyms, antonyms, and words matched
                   with their brief definitions.)

Title: **"Caging Alphabetical Order"**

Purpose: To give children practice in placing words in alphabetical
                   order.

Activity: Game.

Procedure: Divide the class into two teams. The team that can put the
                   animal into the cage first wins a point.

Materials: Make two large cages on the board or on poster board.
                   Place two words, one on each side of the cage. Hand the
                   first person on each team three words (animals). Team

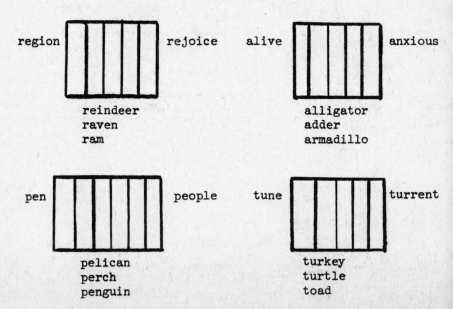

region [   ] rejoice   alive [   ] anxious

      reindeer   alligator
      raven   adder
      ram   armadillo

pen [   ] people   tune [   ] turrent

      pelican   turkey
      perch   turtle
      penguin   toad

members must write the animal in the cage between the other two words in alphabetical order

Title: **"Toss the Ring"**

Purpose: To motivate children to learn their spelling words.

Activity: Game.

Procedure: This is played on a piece of plywood or very heavy cardboard about 18 x 24 inches. With a ruler, mark off a one-inch margin all around the board. Then divide the board into three equal sections across and six equal sections up and down within the margin. Draw lines where you have made the marks. Where each line crosses another, screw in a cup hook. Paint a letter of the alphabet underneath each hook. Since there are 28 hooks, there will be no letters for two of them. Leave these

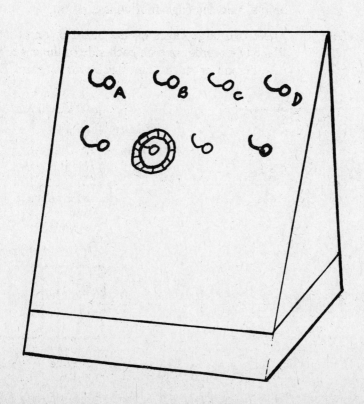

blank, and they can be penalty hooks that everyone should avoid. Make the rings out of sections of clothes-line about eight inches long. Form a ring and fasten ends together with twisted wire or masking tape.

Procedure: The object of the game is to see who is the first one to spell out all the letters of a short word which you have chosen ahead of time.

Title: **"Hear and Show"**

Purpose: To help the students hear word sounds and associate the sounds with their written symbols.

Activity: Game.

Materials: A "sound" holder and cards with the sounds to be studied printed on them.

Procedure: The teacher reads a list of words that begin alike. The students listen for the beginning sound and decide what it is. They then select the card with the right sound on it and place it in the sound holder. The teacher checks to see who has the correct answer. Teams can be formed and points awarded for the right answer.

Illustration: *B*oy *B*ig *B*oat *B*at *B*ay *B*ake *B*ank

Title: **'Game-O"**

Purpose: To reinforce the phonetic sounds of prefixes and suffixes.

Activity: Game.

Materials: Game cards with prefixes and suffixes, bottle caps or buttons.

Procedure: Call words with prefixes or suffixes As in a Bingo game, the students place caps on beginning or ending affixes when words are called out.

G	A	M	E	O
pre	multi	hyper	ad	de
un	micro	sub	di	mis
dis	non	*free*	air	ob
com	en	ab	a	para
in	de	eu	bi	mono

G	A	M	E	O
ing	ship	er	ment	able
ed	est	ly	ness	ous
esce	ary	**free**	ate	hood
ious	ery	ess	sion	tion
ful	ism	ant	ent	tive

Title:	**"Comical Cards"**
Purpose:	To promote correct spelling
Activity:	Game.
Materials:	The current spelling list of words is placed on cards, one set with the correctly spelled words and the other set with incorrect spellings. One set of cards is given to each pair of players.
Procedure:	The dealer distributes the cards. Players then match any pair. such as *receive, recieve, begin, begen,* and place them down with the correctly spelled words on top. If a player puts down a pair with the incorrect spelling on top, the other player takes those cards. The player with the most matched cards correctly placed wins.
Illustration:	

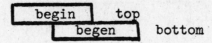

Title:	**"To the Dictionary"**
Purpose:	To increase vocabulary and to practice dictionary skills.
Activity:	Game.
Procedure:	Each child chooses an easy word as, *dog, cat, rat.* Using a dictionary, he prepares a list of words beginning with his chosen word and a clue to each answer. When the pupil gives the clue, the other pupils guess the answer. The first one to guess correctly wins one point. The pupil with the most points is declared the winner for the day.
Example:	Here is an example of using the word *rat.*

1.   A child's toy   rattle
2.   A kind of comb   rattail
3.   A walking stick   rattan

Modified Procedure:	Break students up into small groups. Have each group make up a list of words with clues, then have competition between groups.

Title:	**"Prefix Lotto"**
Purpose:	To provide practice with learning prefixes and their meanings.
Activity:	Game.
Materials:	Lotto cards, as shown in the illustration, with similar and different prefixes on each card. (Each student should have a card.) One clue card, as illustrated, for each prefix used in the game, small pieces of tagboard to cover the prefixes.
Procedure:	Turn the clue cards face down and shuffle them. Have the caller select a card and read the clue aloud. If a player has the corresponding prefix, he may cover it with a small piece of tagboard. The winner must cover all nine prefixes. Some clues, such as "not," may have more than one prefix (un, non, in). Allow each one to be covered when the clue is given.

Player Cards

Prefix Lotto		
pre	dis	trans
un	sub	mis
ex	over	re

Prefix Lotto		
mono	sub	com
non	mis	of
de	inter	epi

Clue Cards

before	not	alone,one	under

Title:	**"Quaker Spelling Meeting"**
Purpose:	To help children to remember how to spell a word.
Activity:	Game.

Procedure: All of the children recite together:

"The Quaker Meeting has begun,
No more laughing, talking or chewing gum."

One child goes to the board and writes the first and last
letters of a word with dashes between them for other
letters. He points to a child to fill in and complete the
word. If he is correct, he chooses another child to fill in
the blanks in the word he chooses.

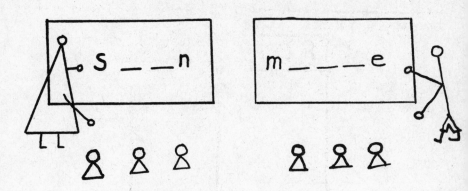

Title: **"Syllable Football'**

Purpose: To provide practice in dividing words into syllables, to
provide practice in determining the accented syllable, to
familiarize the student with the week's new spelling
words.

Activity: Game.

Materials: Spelling list (2 or more syllables).
Large index cards.
Score board (can be drawn on the board).

On the front of the cards are printed the spelling words.
On the back, they are divided into syllables with the
accented syllable designated.

Procedure: 1. The class is divided into two teams and are on opposite
sides of the room.
2. "Kickoff" is determined by a flip of the coin or pick-
ing a number.

CARDS

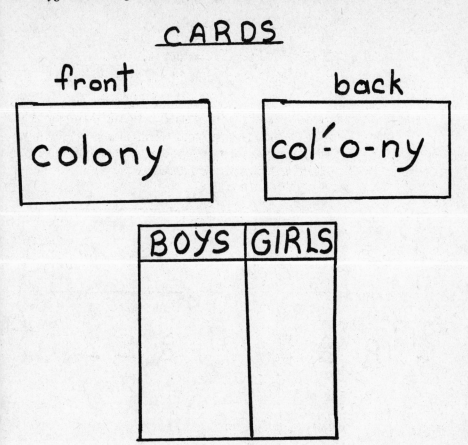

3. The first person on the team which won the toss is shown the front of the card. If he can correctly divide the word into syllables, the team gets a "touchdown" worth 6 points.

4. The same person must identify the accented syllable for the extra point. If he cannot identify it, the other team has a chance to try it. If they identify it, they get the point. If they don't, the cardholder gives the answer, and the point is lost.

5. After one team has attempted or made the touchdown, it is the other team's turn.

6. Proceed in this manner until the word cards have all been shown. The team with the highest score wins.

Title:	**"Sentence Sense"**
Purpose:	This lesson emphasizes dictionary skills and context clues. A child must use his context clues to establish the meaning of the vocabulary word and a dictionary to verify the meaning.
Activity:	Game.
Procedure:	Divide the class into two teams; choose one person to keep score and one to observe the class. At the end of the game, the team with the most points wins.

The teacher will read sentences containing vocabulary words discussed in reading to both teams. In order to score points, a member from one team must indicate if the proper definitions of the vocabulary words were used. The team that has a member who raises his hand first will be recognized. However, the scoring team may be challenged by the other team any time during the game. The team making the challenge must choose a member to use the dictionary and look up the vocabulary word in question. If the team scoring has given the correct answer, they will receive another point and the team challenging will lose a point or vice versa.

Title:	**"Spelling Message"**
Purpose:	To allow spelling practice from the individual's own list.
Activity:	Game.
Materials:	Paper and pencil, small cards with a different letter of the alphabet on each one. There should be one set of the entire alphabet and duplicates of the more commonly used letters.
Procedure:	Place the cards face down and shuffle them. A student selects approximately ten cards and turns them face up, arranging them in order of selection, and leaving a space between each one. (See illustration.) Each student copies the letters and leaves a space between them. He, then, writes a "message," using each letter as an initial letter

for each word. He should endeavor to use as many of his spelling words from his own list as he can to make his message. A five- or ten-minute time limit is sufficient. If students desire, they may read their messages aloud.

Illustration: M_____ D_____ O_____ R_____ T_____ T_____

V_____ A_____ Q_____ N_____

Title: **"Seven-Up"**

Purpose: Can be used to learn spelling words, vocabulary words, or parts of speech.

Activity: Game.

Procedure: Start with eight children, one leader, and seven "tappers." The children at their seats cover their eyes and put their heads down on their desks. Each of the seven children chosen as "tappers" taps one of the seated children.

Then the leader says "Seven-Up" and the children who have been tapped stand. The leader, who has a list of spelling words, has each of the seven standing children spell one of the words. If he correctly spells the word, then he takes the place of the child who tapped him.

Variations: To use with vocabulary words, list the words on the board, then have the leader read a definition to the child who has been tapped and he must give the correct word.

Title: **"Corrective Card Game"**

Purpose: To give the students corrective practice with misspelled words.

Procedure: Pick small groups that have common spelling errors. Write the words (about 6) on a sheet of paper, and with the group spell out and pronounce each word. Beforehand, have the letters printed on cards approximately 3 x 5 inches. The object of the game is to lay out the letters to form the six words. The first player out of cards wins. The dealer shuffles and deals the cards, placing the leftover cards face up in the center. It is the dealer's job to place the "dummy" cards in the proper places. The player on the left begins by laying on the table the starting card for one of the words, and so on around the table. If a child does not have a card to play, he must pass, but he can play as many at a time in as many words as long as they are in order. To save time, another set of words can be printed on the back in another color.

Title:	**"Authors"**
Purpose:	To give practice with prefixes and suffixes. Can be used with verb tenses, etc.
Activity:	Small group game.
Materials:	A set of teacher- or student-made cards. These can be made on 3x5 cards. (See illustration.)
Procedure:	There should be four cards for each root word. For four or five players, 52 cards are needed. (13 root words and 3 derivatives for each.) The object is to form more "books" than any other player. All the cards are dealt out one at a time. The player to the dealer's left begins by laying down a book if he has one. Then he calls a player by name and asks for a specific card. If the person has it, he must hand it over, and the first player has another turn. He may continue asking for specific cards as long as he receives cards. When he fails to get a card, the player to his left takes his turn. The play continues, with books

LIKE	DISLIKE	LIKELY	LIKENESS
like	like	like	like
dislike	dislike	dislike	dislike
likely	likely	likely	likely
likeness	likeness	likeness	likeness

laid down as they are formed, until all the cards have been played. The player with the most books wins.

Title:	**"Tic-Tac-Toe"**
Purpose:	To reinforce spelling words at the end of a unit.
Activity:	Game.
Procedure:	This can be played with small or large groups. Divide into two groups. Draw a large tic-tac-toe grid on the board. The first person on Team 1 is given a word to spell. If he spells it correctly, he goes to the board and puts an X in the square of his choice. The first person on Team 2 then spells a word. If it is spelled correctly, that person puts an 0 in a vacant square. The game proceeds until one team or the "cat" wins, unless someone misspells a word; then that team doesn't get to put a mark on the grid and the other team takes its turn. The children who misspell words are not out of the game, but get their turns as usual in the next round.

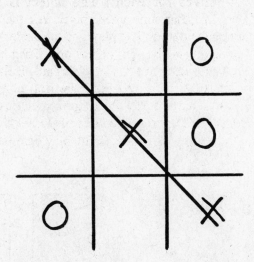

Title:	**"Score a Home Run"**
Purpose:	This exercise is to drill students on prefixes and suffixes.

Activity: Game.

Procedure: Draw three bases and home plate on acetate and on each base put ten (10) words, prefixes, suffixes, or whatever material is to be covered. If the student can successfully master the skill at each base, he scores a home run.

                   This might prove to be a better motivational device than just listing the words or adding prefixes.

Title.   **"Eat the Candy Bar"**

Purpose.   To aid in word spelling.

Activity: Game.

Procedure.   A chair containing five candy bars is placed at the head of

Team #1   Team #2   Team #3   Team #4   Team #5

the room. The children are divided into five teams. The first person in each team must spell a word correctly. If he does, he is allowed to advance one step. If he misses, the next person in line takes his place. The first person to spell all of the words correctly and reach the chair, may eat the candy bar. This is repeated until each person has at least a chance of advancing to the chair.

Title:	**"Anagrams"**
Purpose:	To recognize words through spelling.
Activity:	Game.
Materials:	Outline of basket on flannelboard.
Procedure:	Write the words "Fruits and Vegetables" on the board. Underneath list several common fruits and vegetables in scrambled form. Such as rgeano (orange), mlone (lemon), hqasus (squash), nocr (corn). To the right of these words have a large outline of a basket on a piece of flannelboard. Ask the children "How many of these fruits and vegetables can you put in the basket?" If a child thinks he can unscramble one of the words he

raises his hand and when called upon, writes it on a cardboard strip and sticks it in the basket so that the word shows, but is also in the basket. If he is correct, the word is crossed off the board.

CHAPTER 2

Spelling Instruction with 19
Individualized and Group Activities

In spelling treasure chest 2, independent and group activities are provided to help you individualize your spelling instruction. Group activities are useful for large or small group instruction while the independent activities provide you with the flexibility of meeting individual spelling skill needs of students.

The group activities could be teacher-directed or student-led, permitting you to have more than one instructional group operating simultaneously. For example, you could be leading one group's activities while a student directs another group in another part of the room. At the same time, several other students could be learning spelling by using independent activities. By using these successful teaching activities, you will become adept at manipulating grouping arrangements leading to more precise and effective learning, and your students active involvement will sustain their spelling motivation.

A group activity such as "Mother Goose" could be the instructional activity directed by you while a student is leading another group with "Endings Rule." Still others could be working independently with "Super Speller" and "Animal Words." With this or a similar arrangement, your classroom will buzz with learning excitement not only because the activities are entertaining but because the students' motivation will carry them to the highest and most satisfying reward, the pleasure of learning.

Title:	**'Super Speller''**
Purpose:	To help in spelling the most frequently misspelled words.
Activity:	Independent.
Materials:	Tape recorder and game board.
Procedure:	The student is given a game board which is numbered from one to 25. He also receives a tape recorder which calls out a difficult spelling word, waits 15 or 20 seconds and then spells the word. The recorder can have as many words as the teacher wishes. The student puts a marker on the space marked start. He turns on the tape recorder. If he spells the word correctly in the 15 or 20 seconds, he moves his marker up three spaces. If he misses the word, and the marker is still on start, it remains in position. If the marker has passed start and the student misses, he must move back two places. He must listen to the correct spelling on the recorder before he moves. The student should write the word as he spells it. His goal is to reach "Super Speller."

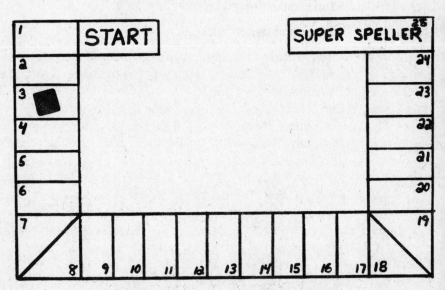

The student spelled the first word correctly
and has moved the marker to the third place.

Title:	**"A Little Spelling Book"**
Purpose:	To aid slow-spellers' spelling skill.
Activity:	Independent.
Materials:	Small pieces of paper with letters of the alphabet. (Several of each letter). Provide pictures and construction paper to make booklets.
Procedure:	Place the alphabet symbols in front of the children. Let them see how many words they can make or give them a word to spell. When they spell a word correctly they can add this word to their "little spelling book." The child can review these periodically and also add words to the booklet. Let the individuals design their booklets as they wish. This will make it more meaningful to the child.

Title:	**"Animal Words"**
Purpose:	To help the students remember difficult spelling words.
Activity:	Independent or group.
Materials:	Paper and magic markers.
Procedure:	The teacher picks out a difficult spelling word for each student. The student is to print the word on a piece of paper with a red magic marker. He makes an animal out of the word with any other color magic marker. The red will make the word stand out. The work can be put on the bulletin board. This activity can be done as a group or individually.

Title:	**"Phonics Posters"**
Purpose:	To insure that each child knows the phonetic sounds represented by consonants.
Activity:	Independent.
Materials:	21 posters, magazines, scissors, glue.
Procedure:	In the first grade, as each consonant is introduced have the children look through the magazines to find a picture that begins with the same sound as the consonant. Cut the picture out and paste it on the poster. Write the letter beside the picture.

Title:	**"Consonant Letters"**
Purpose:	To help children associate consonant letters with speech sounds.
Activity:	Independent.
Materials:	Stack of cards with all the consonant letters of the alphabet on them. One letter to a card.
Procedure:	Cards with the large letters written on them are stacked and placed on a table. A child draws a card from the stack, such as M or H. He then must place the card on something in the room that starts with that sound. For M

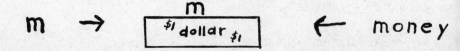

it might be mirror, mitten, mouth, money, or even Mary or Max.

Title:　　**"Halloween Spelling"**

THERE WAS AN OLD

WHO LIVED IN A ROOM

WITH A CROTCHETY

AND A DIRTY

BUT MORE WEIRD THAN THAT

WAS A RED RIVER

WHO SANG TO THE MAN IN THE

MISS WITCH HAS A

WHICH PROUDLY PROTRUDED

FROM A SPOT WHERE HER

　　TOOK A DIP.

SHE SPENT MOST THE DAY

BRUSHING AWAY AT A

THAT STUCK OUT OF HER

HER OF BLACK, OF GREEN,

SPOOKY SIGHT ON HALLOWEEN.

SPELLING LIST

WITCH

ROOM

CAT

TEASPOON

RAT

MOON

WART

NOSE

TOOTH

LIP

HAT

BLACK

GREEN

BONUS LIST

CROTCHETY

WEIRD

PROTRUDED

HALLOWEEN

Purpose: The main objective of this lesson is to present spelling in a motivating manner and, at the same time, teach the children to rhyme.

Activity: Independent.

Materials: Rebus poem and spelling list.

Procedure: Children are to read the poem aloud supplying the proper word for the picture. The pictures may be detachable, enabling children to see correct spelling on reverse side. This subject would be most appropriate around Halloween.

Title: **"Spelling—Addition Anagrams"**

Purpose: To have children put certain words in a sentence together and then think of a new word.

Activity: Independent.

Procedure: Give children the following sentences written either on the board or on ditto, and let them figure out the new word for each sentence. After writing the words, they can look up the answers located at your desk or at another location.

1. Add a trunk of a fallen tree and a novel and get a sailor's bible. (logbook)
2. Add "spying" and a drinking vessel and get what every woman looks at most. (looking glass)
3. Add a great bulk and a plot of land and get a terrible slaughter. (massacre)
4. Add a useful feature of your coat and a literary volume and get a much needed article, especially when filled. (pocketbook)
5. Add a cube of wood and the chief end of man's anatomy, and get a stupid fellow. (blockhead)
6. Add the symbols of ten and fifty and get what every boy should want to do. (XL)
7. Add angry to a verbal effect and get a popular kind of puzzle. (crossword)

8. Add a famous Christmas berry to what trees are made of and get a well known city. (Hollywood)

9. Add judgment to ability and get what people are expected to be at all times. (sensible)

10. Add a fruit to a shepherd dog and get downcast. (melancholy)

Children can make up their own verses to add to the list.

Title:	**"Can You Help Mr. Clown?"**
Purpose:	To develop skills in alphabetizing and spelling.
Activity:	Independent.
Materials:	Ditto sheets containing a clown with balloons containing words.

Mr. Clown needs your help to put his balloons in order.

1. _____ 2. _____ 3. _____ 4. _____
5. _____ 6. _____ 7. _____ 8. _____

Procedure: Put a few words on the board and have the children put them in alphabetical order. Then pass out the ditto sheets and ask them to see if they can help Mr. Clown.

Illustration: On the top of the sheet, it says, "Mr. Clown needs your help to put his balloons in order." Try to write the words in alphabetical order on the bottom of the page. Then color the eight balloons.

Title: **"Word Power"**

Purpose: To develop word building using root words with prefixes and suffixes.

Activity: Group.

Materials: Paper and cardboard strips and a piece of square cardboard.

Procedure: Three strips of paper are made so that they can be moved up and down the squared cardboard. The first strip contains the prefixes, the second contains root words, and the third contains suffixes. By moving the strips up and down, new words can be formed. Words made with prefixes can be checked in the dictionary for correctness and word meaning.

dis un pre	School interest count bend	ed ing s er

Title: **"Stand to Spell"**

Purpose: To develop letter sequence in words.

Activity: Group.

Materials: Construction paper (5" x 11") with letters printed on them (Several letters may need to be duplicated. For example, in the word "Mississippi" the letters "s" and "i" are repeated several times; therefore, several cards would have to be repeated.)

Procedure: The letters are distributed and time is given so that each student will know which letters or letter he has. The teacher or leader will call out a word from a given list. Any one who has a letter contained in the word comes to the front of the room. They arrange themselves in the right order and the rest of the class checks to make sure the spelling of the word is correct.

Title: **"Endings Rule"**

Purpose: To provide students with practice in recognizing word endings and their meanings (suffixes).

Activity: Goup.

Materials: (1) a large circle out of poster board. (2) cards (three per person) with words on them that contain the various endings on the circle.

Procedure: The teacher (or a leader) turns the pointer to one of the endings. Those children who have cards with words ending in the letters that were pointed to, stand by their desks. They then must pronounce the words and use them in a sentence. If a child holds up the wrong card, or mispronounces it, or cannot explain or demonstrate its meaning, he must keep the card. The leader takes the cards from the children whose responses are correct. This continues until some child is without cards. He then becomes the leader.

The words that are used could be a combination of students' spelling list, review words that they should have known from the previous year, and possibly some of the vocabulary words from a reading lesson that all the students have already had.

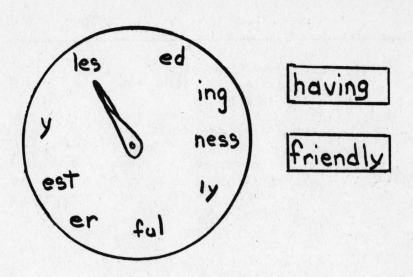

Title:	**"Mother Goose"**
Purpose:	Spelling power development.
Activity:	Group.
Materials:	Draw a clock diagram on the board or a transparency with the letters MOTHER GOOSE arranged on it. Begin anywhere on the clock and mix the letters up.
Procedure:	Tell the child you want him to see how many words he can make from the letters found in the words MOTHER GOOSE. Give some definitions of the words you can find. Below are some examples:

                                                                ANSWERS

1. A June flower   1. rose
2. Foot covering   2. shoe
3. To lie quietly   3. rest
4. In that place   4. there
5. Very warm   5. hot

6.	Part of a plant in the ground	6.	root
7.	A precious stone	7.	gem
8.	Not too long	8.	short
9.	To look	9.	see
10.	A cow says	10.	moo
11.	An insect that eats woolen clothes	11.	moth
12.	A part of your foot	12.	toe
13.	To decay	13.	rot
14.	To say hello	14.	greet
15.	A place where we buy things	15.	store
16.	An animal that roots in the mud	16.	hog
17.	Also	17.	too
18.	Where hens rest at night	18.	roost
19.	A very brave man	19.	hero
20.	A very large deer (Bullwinkle is one)	20.	moose
21.	In this place	21.	here
22.	Spook	21.	ghost
23.	Two and one are =	23.	three
24.	Where you live	24.	home
25.	An animal you can ride	25.	horse

Title:	**"Guide Word Practice"**
Purpose:	To teach the dictionary skills of using guide words.
Activity:	Group.
Materials:	Dictionaries and duplicated sheets.
Procedure:	Have students cross out all words on the duplicated sheets that are not found between the guide words on a given page in a dictionary. They then alphabetize the rest.

Example: Using the guide words—"tool box" to "torque"

toothless	torpid	tortoise
top hat	topography	toolroom
tongue-tied	torpedo	topaz
topknot	toothpick	tonight
tornado	torch	totem pole

Title: **"I Am Thinking of a Word"**

Purpose: To practice spelling words, orally.

Activity: Group.

Materials: A list of spelling words to be learned.

Procedure: A child stands in front of the group and says, "I am thinking of a word." He chooses a child to guess the word. The chosen child says, "Is the word cat, c-a-t?"

The leader says, "No, it is not cat, c-a-t." He chooses another child to spell a word until someone spells the one the leader has chosen.

Both the leader and the child chosen are getting spelling practice.

Title: **"Prefix Meanings"**

Purpose: To understand the meaning of prefix.

Activity: Group.

Materials: Posterboard, magic markers, string, brads, ruler, and pencil.

Procedure: Define what a prefix is. Place posterboard against the blackboard. Ask for a volunteer to come up to the front and match the colored string by the prefixes to the definition of prefixes. After each match, ask the class to give you a word which has that prefix in it.

Illustration: A prefix is at the beginning of a word; to fix or put before or in front.

PREFIXES

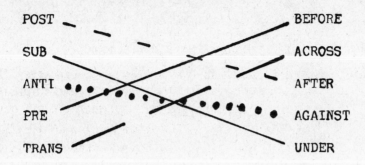

POST	BEFORE
SUB	ACROSS
ANTI	AFTER
PRE	AGAINST
TRANS	UNDER

Title: **"Toss and Spell"**

Purpose: Development of skills in spelling.

Activity: Group.

Materials: Bean bags, board, spelling words on 3 x 5 cards. (These words will change in time from development of vocabulary and in connection with stories studied.) The words should include some difficult ones and some easy ones.

8	5
7	2
	9
10	3
1	6

Procedure:	The board is placed an equal distance from each group. Groups alternate. The leader from each group tosses the bean bag. The teacher then draws a word from the spelling word stack. If the leader spells the word correctly, the team gets the points shown on the toss board. He then goes to the end of the line. If he misses the word, then no points are given and he goes to the end of the line. The teacher can call time or can remove the cards spelled correctly and the game is over with the team scoring the most points the winner.
Illustration:	(Suggestion for design of board)

Title:	**"Homonyms, Antonyms, and Synonyms"**
Purpose:	To teach students the homonyms, antonyms, and synonyms.
Activity:	Group.
Materials:	A piece of posterboard is used to hold the word cards. It is divided into three sections with a heading of Homonym, Antonym, and Synonym over each section.

Poster

Homonym	Antonym	Synonym
air heir	tall Short	Small Little
very vary	slow fast	halt stop

Small folds are used to hold the cards on which are written the appropriate words. Word cards are made for each section.

Procedure: For each two words held in a fold, one should be held up and the instructor say, "Find a synonym (homonym or antonym) for this word." The first child to find it scores a point or receives some kind of response in praise of his correct answer.

Having opposite-colored word cards for each section also helps the child know that word goes in an opposite one that is already placed in a slot. The different colors may be switched, also, to get more variety in words.

Title: **"Spelling Hang Up"**

Purpose: To provide an enjoyable spelling review for the children and to develop an audio-visual concept of their words.

Activity: Group.

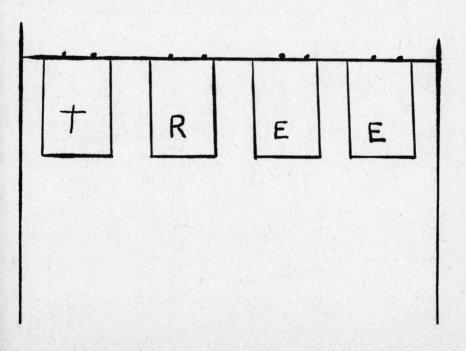

Materials: String a line drawn across the front of the room and clip on several clothespins. Make large cards and write the letters of the alphabet on them, one letter per card.

Procedure: Give each child a card, distributing all 26 cards. If there are more than 26 children, pass out extra vowel cards labeled a_2, e_2, etc. Also extra vowels could be given to children holding seldom used letters such as "x" or "z." The teacher calls out a word from the spelling review list, and the children, holding the letter cards needed to spell the word, quickly run to the line and hang up the word by placing the letters in correct sequence. The other children in the room judge the correctness of the spelling. For variety, call out a prefix or suffix to the word hung up or substitutions can be made, such as after "tree" has been hung up, tell them to change it to "bee."

Title: **"Teaching A Generalization"**

Purpose: To help students learn inductively the spelling generalization: "i" is usually written before "e" except after "c" when the long sound of "e" is produced.

Activity: Group.

Materials: Overhead projector and transparencies.

Procedure: 1. Motivate the students to spell well through the use of a business letter asking for a part-time job which will augment an allowance. Students will locate errors in the letter and discuss why or why not the boy got the job.

          2. Place a list of words before them. Ask them to pronounce the words and tell what sound the vowels have.

          3. The students will look at the words and notice the letter that precedes the "ie" or "ei."

          4. Students will list what letters precedes the vowels.

Illustration:	*Before "ei"*	*Before "ie"*
	c (deceive)	l (believe)
	c (conceit)	p (piece)
	c (receipt)	l (relief)
		s (siege)
		r (priest)

Discuss the findings and make the generalizations collectively.

CHAPTER 3

How to Build Oral Communication Skills with 40 Activities

As you are aware, oral communication skills are the solid foundation upon which all language skills are built. Whether the skills are receptive or expressive, speaking and listening are of prime importance, and the acquisition of these skills by children bears directly on their reading and writing skills. Even though children come to school with oral communication abilities, further development and refinement of these skills are most important and are a major part of the primary language arts program.

You may have available in your classroom language arts texts containing suggestions for teacher-directed instruction for oral language development. Needless to say, these are appropriate lessons, but notably insufficient in number to permit you to administer sufficient dosage to those with poorly developed oral vocabularies, such as the culturally disadvantaged children who should be more precisely labeled linguistically deprived.

If your students do not have language arts textbooks, then these oral communication activities will not be just valuable supplementary helpers, but could become the substantive backbone of your oral communication curriculum.

Even intermediate grade teachers will find useful ideas in this chapter for meeting specific speaking and listening deficiencies observed in some of their students. There is no question that some intermediate children could profitably spend time improving their oral communication abilities which would have transfer of learning effect on their reading and writing skills, because oral communication is the foundation for all the language skills.

The contents of this chapter include group and independent activities to help you facilitate your students' oral language development. Most of the activities are used with groups because the nature of the skill necessitates speakers having audiences who in turn are using their listening skills. Additionally, because children's listening skill ability is, unfortunately, frequently taken for granted, a number of group listening activities are provided separately from the oral communication ideas, enabling you to select specific listening developmental activities when you need to focus instruction toward developing this skill. And, although the group activities are interesting to children and are usually considered fun activities, I have, nevertheless, included game ideas for listening development to expand your teaching options further.

Start using these ideas a few at a time and see how lively and productive your oral language program becomes.

Title:	**"Word Back"**
Purpose:	To develop listening skill.
Activity:	Game.
Materials:	Blackboard, chalk.
Procedure:	Teacher divides class into two teams. The first member of one team gives a word. The first member of the other team must give a rhyming word. Then the next team member of the other team gives another rhyming word. This goes on until no more rhyming words can be given. A point is scored when a team cannot give a word back. The teacher or a student writes words on the blackboard.
Illustration:	Team I Team II
	red head
	said thread

Title:	**"Listening Relay"**
Purpose:	To improve listening habits.

Activity:	Game.
Materials:	Chalkboard.
Procedure:	First have the students count off by four's so that there are four equal teams. The teams should stand in front of the chalk board facing away from it. The teacher tells the first member of each team to perform some task. This is whispered so no one else can hear. The message is relayed until the last member has received it. He then performs the activity on the board if so instructed.
Illustration:	"Write the name of the teacher you had last year in manuscript without capital letters." "Write your name and address on the board omitting every other letter." "Draw three circles approximately one foot in diameter with all three circles touching one another." After the last pupil has completed his instruction, he moves to the front of the line. Points can be awarded for correct responses to add competitive spirit.

Title:	**"What Do You See?"**
Purpose:	To encourage oral expression and creative thinking.
Activity:	Independent.
Materials:	Peekbox and tape recorder.
Procedure:	Arrange the peekbox on a table next to a tape recorder. Ask a student to look in the box and tell a story about what he sees into the tape recorder. When he is finished, he can listen to his story and perhaps share it with the class. This can also help the teacher (by listening) to detect language errors.

Title:	**"Descript-O"**
Purpose:	To develop the ability to speak orally and to give accurate descriptions.
Activity:	Independent.

Procedure:	Each student is given materials to create a collage. The collage needs to represent something that can be given a description. After the collages are finished, display them around the room, without students' names attached. Each student will come before the class and describe his collage so that others will know which one it is. The student will discuss any particular meaning that the collage has.

Title:	**"Mirror, mirror . . ."**
Purpose:	Oral communication.
Activity:	Independent.
Materials:	Mirror.
Procedure:	Child stands in front of the class and holds the mirror so that he can see himself but so as not to prevent the other children from seeing him. The child proceeds to tell who he is and what he looks like to himself.
	Each child has a chance to tell his interests as well as physical characteristics.

Title:	**"Interviewing and Reporting"**
Purpose:	To give children practice talking to improve their oral language skills.
Activity:	Individual and Group.
Procedure:	The children are asked to interview their parents or grandparents about the ways in which they think we live better than they did. Then the children can share some of the more interesting stories with the class.
Illustration:	Interview question samples:
	What were the cars and airplanes like? What did children do for fun? How were clothes different? What was different about the schools?

Title:	**"Mysterious Object"**
Purpose:	To teach children to listen, think, and follow directions.
Activity:	Group.
Materials:	Paper and scissors for each child.
Procedure:	Say "Take out a sheet of paper and scissors. Fold the paper the short way with the lines so that the corners are even. Hold the paper so that the open side is up. Now, starting at the bottom on the right corner, cut a half circle so you end on the left bottom corner. We have a little hut but it doesn't have a door or windows. Why don't we cut a door in the middle about 2 inches high and ½ inch wide? This doesn't have to be exact so do not measure it. The hut is looking better but it still isn't finished. Add another door to the right of the first door only make it small, approximately ½" x ½". Now punch a hole through both sides of the hut in the middle of the right side and cut out a little window. The window will be above and to the right of the little door."

Afterward, the students are told to open their papers, whereupon they will find they have a jack-o-lantern.

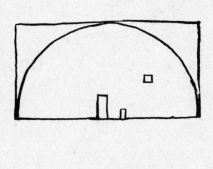 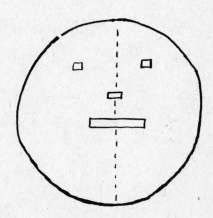

Title:	**"Can You Guess the Sound?"**
Purpose:	Development of listening skills.

Activitity:	Group.
Materials:	Tape recorder with different sounds taped on it.
Procedure:	Use the tape recorder to record the different sounds (tapping on a window, knocking on a door, tearing paper, popping corn), then have the children listen and imagine what the sound is. They can draw what they think they hear.

Title:	**"Listening Detectives"**
Purpose:	To develop better listening and identification of sentence parts.
Activity:	Group.
Materials:	Chalk board, pencil and paper, paragraphs.
Procedure:	On the chalkboard have six columns labeled: who, what, why, when, where, and how. Have several students come to the front to fill out the board and have everyone else write at their desks. As you read a paragraph slowly and distinctly to them, have the students fill in as they detect the various questions (who, when, why, etc.) asked. Change the students at the board after each paragraph.

Title:	**"Magic Picture"**
Purpose:	To develop better listening habits.
Activity:	Group.
Materials:	Graph paper. Picture with prepared directions (may be on a tape recorder).
Procedure:	The students are given paper with lines (graph paper or make your own with larger squares, for young children). Directions are given where to place a dot. Then the directions for the next one are given, etc. The directions may be given like this:

two squares down—three across.

When two dots are given a line may be drawn to connect the dots this prevents confusion at the end. The children may want to color the picture and a bulletin board may be made with pictures being displayed.

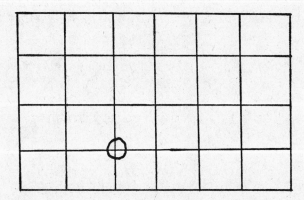

Title:	**"Shake a Sound"**
Purpose:	To develop students' use of effective listening.
Activity:	Group.
Materials:	Two containers of identical ingredients, example: rocks, rice, buttons, marbles, paper clips, nails, salt, etc.
Procedure:	Fill the containers, glue or tape them shut. You could paint them to be more colorful but paint them all the same color so players don't get confused with matching color instead of sound. You really need only three or four pairs of containers. To play the game, let one or more students shake the sound and try to find a perfect match. They shake one container, listen, and then, trying to keep the sound in their head, match it with another container that they feel is the same sound. Containers you might use are flip-top bandage boxes, tobacco tins, film cans, etc.

Title:	**"Look, Listen, Learn"**
Purpose:	To develop the listening skills.

Activity: Group.

Materials: Large sheet of cardboard and some animal stories and poems.

Procedure: Before you play this listening-looking game, it's a good idea to read animal stories and poems to the children. Next, have children sit in a semi-circle with their eyes closed. Choose a child to go behind the screen (large piece of cardboard) and imitate the sound of an animal. The other children must identify not only the animal sound, but also the child who is doing the imitating.

Title: **"Fact or Opinion"**

Purpose: To develop listening skills by distinguishing between fact and opinion statements.

Activity: Group.

Procedure: Have the students listen to some sentences taken from the daily newspaper. Have them decide if they are fact or opinion and why. Then let them guess where the article came from—what section of the paper.

Illustration: *"Goodbye Columbus* is the warmest, friendliest, most huggable film I've seen in a long time." *Entertainment Section*—opinion—the author needs to give some supporting reasons.

"Over a period of four years, the Navy spent $375,000 in a scientific study of Frisbees to see if the flight characteristics of these plastic toys could somehow be adapted for warfare. *Fact.* From page 1. This can be verified from records.

Title: **"From Here To There"**

Purpose: To increase vocabulary and advance listening skills.

Activity: Group.

Materials: A train with the "cars" made from different colored construction paper, a black construction paper railroad track that runs all over the walls, train schedule for each student. Begin the train at the place called Here. Along the way have stations entitled Wordsville, Vocabulary Station, Lollipop Place, etc. (Let the students name the places.) The destination is the place called, There.

Procedure: Begin the train with a new word on the engine and one on the caboose with no cars in between. Pronounce the words for the students, but do not give them the definitions unless they especially ask for them. Have the students listen for the words, during the day, as you use them in context, so they will get an idea of the meaning; or, you may want to give a "built-in" definition. For example, "Some bears hibernate; that is, they sleep during the winter.

Alert listeners will recognize the words as "train" words. Each day the train grows as the engine is moved up and 2 or 3 "cars" are added. Soon it will stretch from Here to There!

Let each student keep his own train schedule. If he hears the words used, understands their meaning, and/or uses them correctly in oral or written communication, he has arrived at a certain point toward his destination, There. For example, if the engine is at Lollipop Place, and the student knows all of the words in the train, from the engine to the caboose, he can mark the arrival date on his train schedule.

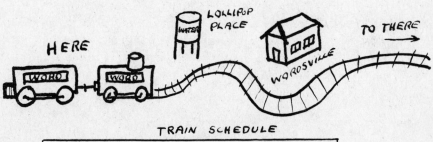

TRAIN SCHEDULE

ARRIVAL			
PLACE	DATE	PLACE	DATE

Title:	**"Speak and Listen to One Another"**
Purpose:	Help develop oral communication skills of listening and speaking.
Activity:	Group.
Materials:	Strips of paper with famous characters on them.
Procedure:	One child receives a character and tells the class whatever he wants to about it. The other characters are given out one at a time. When that is accomplished, pass the same strips out again, one at a time, and have these children tell what they remember of what the other children said This can only be done through listening to one another. You must listen, but you also must talk.

Jack and Jill	Santa Claus
Mother Goose	Peter Rabbit

Title:	**"Dial a Topic"**
Purpose:	To provide practice in creative oral expression.
Activity:	Group.
Materials:	Circular Dial-A-Topic.

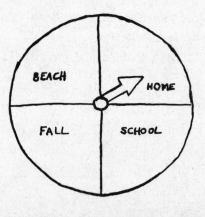

DIAL - A - TOPIC

Procedure: Have each group (4 or 5 per group) form a circle. The captain of the team spins the dial and wherever it stops, that's the topic to discuss with the captain. Start off with the captain, and others carry on around the circle.

Title: **"Telephone Communication"**

Purpose: To provide practice in proper use of the telephone and *Oral Communication*.

Activity: Group.

Materials: Borrow practice telephones (standard and pay) from Telephone Company. Also available are film strips, and charts regarding telephone usage.

Procedure: Discuss and list any suggestions students make about telephone conversations; i.e. courtesy, how to dial, taking messages for Mom, Dad, etc.

Title: **"Introduce Me"**

Purpose: To provide oral communication practice in interviewing and making introductions.

Activity: Group.

Procedure: (To be done at beginning of school year.) Let students find partners. Provide a three-minute period for each to interview the other, finding out his name, where he lives, his ambition or favorite hobby.

     Then all students, in turn, introduce the person they interviewed. But they must look directly at that seated person and introduce him with one good sentence.

     This will help the speaker to develop eye-to-eye contact and to organize his thoughts and words.

Title: **"Telephoning"**

Purpose: To motivate children to practice oral communication skills in a realistic, simulated situation.

Activity: Begin with class and then to pairs.

Materials: Telephone usage booklets, 2 toy telephones, yarn, paper (colored construction), colored chalk, 2 small paper sacks and illustration board (for telephone do's).

Procedure: After the children are given a booklet on how to use the telephone correctly, read and discuss it in the class. Then either the teacher or the class can decorate the bulletin board with a boy and a girl talking on the telephone.

Use a yarn cord for each phone—running from the phone to receiver. At the end of each cord have a small paper phone. Attach to each phone a small paper sack. In these

sacks, place several different topic headings such as animals, sports, books, history, science, hobbies, etc. On a table under the bulletin board place two toy telephones. Here the children can practice their telephone skills while talking about different topics.

Above the bulletin board, place a card (illustration board), with important telephone do's—so the children will have a helpful reminder when practicing.

Title:	**"Combating Stage Fright"**
Purpose:	To help the student overcome self-consciousness, shyness, being tongue-tied, or any of the manifestations of "stage fright".
Activity:	Group.
Procedure:	Advise students to begin their speech with something funny, a joke, an anecdote, etc., to relax the speaker and audience.

Help the students to select a topic of genuine interest to them: thinking about the topic will help them forget their anxiety.

Advise rehearsing the talk, but not *memorizing* it. Fear of forgetting contributes to fright.

Choose a controversial subject for discussion, something everyone will have an opinion on.

Have a *Tall-Tale Contest*: To help the students forget themselves, see who can tell the tallest tale. Even the students who normally have nothing to say can participate in something which is only make-believe, especially since they have no fear of making a mistake.

Title:	**"Open-ended Questions"**
Purpose:	To help children develop oral communication skills.
Activity:	Group.
Procedure:	These questions are meant to be controversial, with neither a correct nor an incorrect solution; the type of

problem on which everyone should have an opinion. There should be discussion from all students, thereby giving even students who normally have nothing to say an opportunity to speak.

Given the question, the class could be divided into smaller discussion groups, each with a secretary to record the pros and cons. After a set period of time, the group would stop expressing opinions and review and summarize their position, then report to the class as a whole.

This would be an excellent opportunity for the teacher to tape-record the class in conversation to discover oral language errors.

Illustrations: What is a good excuse? . . . . . a bad excuse? Why use excuses? When do you use them?

What's a hero?

What makes a punishment fair or unfair?

What do you think about . . . . ?

Title:	**"Goofies"**
Purpose:	To encourage creative expression.
Activity:	Group—Independent.
Materials:	A.Poems—"Eletephony," "Kangarooster," "Octopussy," or any other article about an animal in a different fashion than it is usually thought of.
	B.Paper, pencil, and crayons.
	C.Large book entitled, "Our Big Book of Goofies."
Procedure:	Read the poems or stories to the children to introduce the lesson. Discuss with them why these animals' names are "goofy" and how other foolish names can be created. Then direct them to create, draw, and color their own "Goofies" and to give them names. Provide a time to let the children share their originals. After they have completed this activity, tell them to save their "Goofies" and during free time to write a story or poem to accompany them. Explain that a "Goofie" book will be made for the reading table and each person in the class will put his

favorite (or favorites) in the book when he has completed it. The book will then be available in the future for everyone to enjoy reading.

My Pigider,
Is Quite A Biter,
But When He Spins,
He Ends Up Tighter.

Title:	**"Choral Reading"**
Purpose:	To encourage growth in learning to speak with clear, rhythmic voices.
Activity:	Group.
Materials:	A book of poems that have familiar words and easily recognizable rhythms.
Procedure:	At first, the teacher may read the poem through to familiarize the class with the theme. She may then have the students read the poem orally. A poem with dialogue may be divided as such: children with deeper voices may portray big, gruff characters, such as giants, monsters, large animals. Children with light, soft voices may speak as fairies, butterflies, small animals, etc. When the class has accomplished a good production of the poem, they may want to perform for parents, another class, or a school function.

Illustration:	*The Owl and The Pussycat* is a good poem for dialogue content. The owl's lines would be read by the boys, and the pussycat's by the girls.

Title:	**"Morning News Report"**
Purpose:	To develop speaking abilities.
Activity:	Group.
Procedure:	At the beginning of each day, five different children present news coverage. The teacher can set up a table and chair for the news commentator. The mini-news report mocks the ones on T. V. The weather report, school news, sports, current events, and the editoral are examples of topics which may be covered.

Title:	**"Which Picture?"**
Purpose:	To provide practice in using oral language.
Activity:	Group.
Materials:	Several large mounted pictures on the chalk tray which can be easily described.
Procedure:	One person is chosen to be IT. He mentally chooses a picture and then describes it, being sure to keep his eyes on the class, not on the picture. The first child to guess which picture is being described gets to be the next IT. Proceed until everyone has had a chance to be IT.
	Alternate Procedure: When a person has been the leader once, he may guess again and, if right, he may choose a player to give the next description.
	Pictures drawn by the children could be used. Pictures related to a unit of work, holidays, or important events might be employed.

Title:	**"Projecting To Inanimate Objects"**
Purpose:	To motivate children to use oral expression.

Activity:	Group.
Materials:	Cards containing the names of household articles (can opener, TV, bed, water faucet).
Procedure:	Students will draw a card and pretend they are the household item, acting out a day in the life of the item.
Example:	"Hello, I'm Mr. Refrigerator. Some people call me Mr. Clean because I'm so white. I'm a hummer because I hum all day. Everyone takes advantage of me, always poking inside me. I get tired of having my cubes rattled and giving up my salad. Wouldn't you? But at least I'm cool, unless you leave my door open. Take care of me."

Title:	**"Translating Pictures into Words"**
Purpose:	Oral expression.
Activity:	Group or independent.
Materials:	Pictures.
Procedure:	Give each group of three to five students a color scene from your picture file. Let each group try to say in words exactly what the picture said with color or form. This is a real challenge and popular with the children.
	Use picture post cards of a group of states. Allow the children to work alone or in pairs to make one good sentence summarizing and describing the pictured scene.
	If your children are "lean" in words, why not work on the same cards using an opaque projector so that everyone can see?
	Another day, reverse the process and let the class paint pictures to match their own descriptive paragraphs. Similarly, have the children translate action pictures into action sentences.

Title:	**"Picture Stimulus"**
Purpose:	To stimulate oral language development.
Activity:	Group.

Procedure: Write a word such as "slush" on the board. Ask several
                 students to tell immediately what picture it evokes in
                 their imagination. Choose other words and continue in
                 the same manner. Show the students a picture and ask
                 them pertinent questions: What is happening? Why?
                 What do you think will happen next? Does it remind you
                 of anything that ever happened to you? Proceed to other
                 pictures and ask the students to supply the story and
                 details to round out the scene.

Title: **"Puppet Introduction"**

Purpose: To learn the proper ways of introducing people to one
                 another.

Activity: Group.

Materials: Simple hand puppets, one for each student. Each puppet
                 should represent a certain type of person. For example,
                 one can be a policeman, one an older lady, one a princi-
                 pal, etc.

Procedure: Call on students at random to introduce their puppets to
                 each other properly.

Title: **"Five Little Pumpkins Sitting on a Gate"**

Purpose: The development of oral language at Halloween time.

Activity: Group.

Procedure: Teach the whole class the poem. Use five different
                 pumpkin faces and have five children say the individual
                 lines.

             "Five Little Pumpkins Sitting On A Gate"
         Five little pumpkins sitting on a gate.
         The first one said, "Oh, my it's getting late."
         The second one said, "There are witches in the air."
         The third one said, "Well, I don't care."
         The fourth one said, "Let's run and run and run."
         The fifth one said, "I'm ready for some fun!"

Whoo-oo went the wind
And out went the lights
And the five little pumpkins rolled out of sight.

Title:	**"Poetry"**
Purpose:	Development of creative expression.
Activity:	Group.
Materials:	Ditto sheets containing several poems with directions for choral reading and tape recorder.
Procedure:	Explain the directions for choral reading and assign the parts to certain pupils. Put on the tape recorder after they have practiced it once. Tape the choral reading and then play it back for the class.
Illustration:	Jonathan Bing

All: Poor old Jonathan Bing
Went out in his carriage to visit the King.

Girls: But everyone pointed and said, "Look at that! Johnathan Bing has forgotten his hat!"

Boys: (He'd forgotten his hat!)

Title:	**"Advertising Specials"**
Purpose:	To develop oral communication skills and children's ability to think up creative descriptions and slogans to advertise a product of their choice.
Activity:	Group.
Materials:	This is left up to the student. He can make whatever materials he feels he needs to advertise his product, or he can bring the actual product to class.
Procedure:	Students will be asked to choose products they have seen advertised or they can make up their own original product that serves some purpose. They will try to think up slogans and other devices to advertise their product to the class. The advertisements should be limited to one minute. The object is to make their product sound so good that someone in the class would like to buy it.
	A variation would be to already have ten or 15 items on a table, and have students come up one at a time and, on the spur of the moment, tell as much about the product as they can.
	If a video-tape machine is available, you can video-tape the students as they advertise their products and then play it back for them to see.
Title:	**"Use of Telephone"**
Purpose:	To learn how to call the proper authorities in an emergency or time of need.
Activity:	Group.
Materials:	Telephone and telephone numbers of fire station, police, etc.
Procedure:	Class discussion of necessary information to give when making an emergency phone call. Each student is given an address, according to where he is seated (for example, Table 1, Seat 2). One child is chosen to be the Fireman and turns his back to the class. Teacher chooses a student whose "House Is On Fire." Another student is chosen to make a call and report the fire, giving all the necessary information. The Fireman finds the fire and puts it out.

This game can also be used to report an accident or other incidents.

Title:	**"Freeze"**
Purpose:	Development of oral communication skills.
Activity:	Group.
Procedure:	Directions to the class: When I say FREEZE, you are to stop work in whatever position you are in. If you are putting on your coat for recess, you must FREEZE. If you are clearing your desk, you must FREEZE.
	Then I'll pick someone (often a quiet student) to describe someone. The person described can then go on with what he was doing.

Title:	**"T.V. and Imagination"**
Purpose:	Development of oral communication skills.
Activity:	Group.
Materials:	All students need a T.V. at home.
Procedure:	Directions to group: This week I'd like you to watch television a new way. Fix the T.V. so you can see the picture but cannot hear what is said.
	This week I'd like you to watch the first half of the _____ show. We will talk about the show in school. Try to understand without hearing the talking, what the show is about.
	If a child cannot visualize from what he hears, try asking that child to listen to a favorite T.V. show with the sound on and the picture off.
	A note home to the parents should be written explaining the purpose of this activity!

Title:	**"Opinions Please"**
Purpose:	Development of oral communication.

Activity: Group.

Materials: Obtain as many toy and department store catalogs as possible. The students need different colored crayons.

Procedure: Directions to class: Here are several catalogs I'm sure you will enjoy looking through. I'm going to give each of you a color. When you find a catalog you enjoy, tell me. Then I'll ask you to go through the catalog and decide what you like best on each page. You will put a circle in your color around the things you like best. I wish you could have all the things you like, but it will be fun just to pretend.

Variations:

1. During indoor recess days, let two children look through the catalog together and discuss the things they like. Putting a verbal child with a quiet one might help.
2. One student could name things on the pages and ask the remedial student to repeat the names.
3. Have the students copy the names of the item and also the page number where it was found.
4. Have each student write a paragraph trying to sell an article that he prefers.

Title: **"Practice Making Introductions"**

Purpose: To build listening ability

Activity: Group

Materials: Several slips of paper containing unusual names

Procedure: Give each child a secret name on a piece of paper. He is to show it to no one. Go to Pupil No. 1, read his secret name and bring him up to Pupil No. 2. Introduce them, using their new names. Bring Pupil No. 1 up to Pupil No. 3 and introduce them, looking at each secret name as you do. After you have introduced No. 1 to No. 4, then leave him on his own to introduce these three children to the rest of the class. No. 1 will use secret names only for Pupils Nos. 2, 3, and 4. He will use the real names of the rest of the classmates. The listening practice will come when the first introductions are made. If you run out of time before each person has a chance to introduce three new names to the class, keep a record where you left off, so you can begin there next time. Once the rest of the class sees how much trouble Pupil No.1 has remembering the new names of No. 2, 3, and 4, they will be extra attentive in order to hear and remember the secret names.

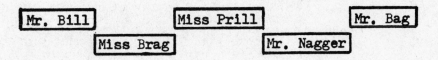

Mr. Bill	Miss Prill	Mr. Bag
Miss Brag	Mr. Nagger	

Title:	**"Describing Characters"**
Purpose:	To give practice in speaking and listening.
Activity:	Group.
Materials:	Paper and pencil for each child.
Procedure:	Have pupils write a three-sentence or shorter description of a familiar story, (nursery rhyme, fairy tale) telling incidents, but not naming names. Let each child read his condensed story to the class and call on someone to guess what it is. Then that person can be next.
Illustration:	There was a house in the woods. A little golden-haired girl came in and ate from three bowls on the table. The owners of the house were upset when they returned (Goldilocks and the Three Bears).

Title:	**"Informal Talking"**
Purpose:	Discussion opportunities.
Activity:	Group.
Procedure:	Tell a story about somebody who was afraid of something. Start talking about fears. Tell the children one thing you used to be afraid of as a child. Give the details of just how you felt about this fear. Tell how you got over it. Together, make a list on the board to help children remember what they are going to talk about.
	What I'm afraid of

Why?
How I feel
What I imagine when I'm scared
What I do to fight my fear

Round-Table Discussion:

Choose from a box a subject such as these:

What parents don't understand.
The teachers I like best.
What I can do at home to make it a better place.
The rules that could make bicycle riders safe in this town.

Ask the children to contribute topics to this box.

Discuss the topics.

Title:	**"Talking People"**
Purpose.	Development of oral communication.
Activity:	Small group.
Materials.	Several sets of paper dolls. Have the remedial students punch them out and cut out their clothes. To do this activity, pick children in the remedial group who are generally quiet and need encouragement to join in discussions. Some children may be able to bring paper dolls from home. (Children can be encouraged to make their own puppets out of socks, etc.)
Procedure:	Here are some paper dolls we are going to use as puppets. You may dress them as you like. If you can make up a play for your puppets, that will be fine. If you cannot, use the topics I have written on the board for you. Make your puppets talk about the topics.
	Let's read the topics together. You will have to speak the part for each person in your play. After we get good at this, we will let you be three people and later, if you like, you can pick a partner and each one take a part.

Play Topics:

1. A child wants some candy before dinner and mother says no.

2. A child wants to watch a T.V. show after his bedtime and his mother asks why.
3. A child doesn't want to eat some food his mother insists he eat.
4. Two children are talking about some money they lost on the way to school.
5. A mother is telling a detective that her car is missing.
6. Two children are lost in a big city park and do not know what to do.
7. Two children are staying together overnight and are talking about school.

Raise your hand if you want to do a topic. If you have a better topic, let me discuss it with you before you present it to the class.

If you wish, you can tape your puppets to rulers and make some sets for your play. Make your play as exciting as you can.

CHAPTER 4

21 Handwriting Activities That
Help to Insure Legibility

Teaching children handwriting skills has never been more important than today because the need for communication skills is increasing. Our technological society demands more and better communication. Yet, there has been a decline in handwriting instruction as compared with the early quarter of the 20th century with the inevitable consequence that the quality of handwriting has lessened. As teachers, we are responsible for reversing this decline in handwriting quality.

Surveys of teachers indicate that only about half of them teach handwriting systematically. Would one principal cause be the dull routine followed or inflicted on elementary students? Now you can do something to overcome that problem because in this chapter you will find 21 successful handwriting activities. Everyone is functional and yet interesting. Not only will your students enjoy them, but you will find them pleasing to present.

Individualizing your instruction to meet student handwriting needs is as important as in any other subject area. To help you accomplish this task, the 21 successful handwriting activities are divided into independent and group classifications. When some students need individual reinforcement, you will have available independent activities, and the group activities are usable for small or large groups.

The purpose of each activity will indicate whether the handwriting practice will be manuscript or cursive. However, most activities could be used for either manuscript or cursive skill development, making them usable in both primary and intermediate grades. Occasionally use manuscript activities in the upper grades for skill maintenance.

Systematic, sequential handwriting instruction will facilitate legible writing skill. With these 21 ideas, you will be able to sustain motivation and interest of your pupils.

===

Title: **"Find the Secret Message"**

Purpose: To give some practice with manuscript writing.

Activity: Independent.

Manuscript: A copy of the following puzzle.

T	h	i	s			i	s		m	y
₁T	₅h	₇i	₂S			₇i	₂S		₆m	₃Y
				₁₃V	₄e	₈r	₃Y			
₁₁b	₄e	₂S	₁₀t							
				₁₂W	₆r	₇i	₁₀t	₇i	₉n	₁₄g

1. T	5. h	9. n	13. v
2. S	6. m	10. t	14. g
3. Y	7. i	11. b	
4. e	8. r	12. w	

_____   _____   _____   _____

_____   _____   _____   _____

write message above

Procedure: Read the title and explain that to find the secret message, the children have to look at the numeral in the first box, find that numeral below and write the letter in the correct box. The letter must be written well. After they have completed this, have them write the message on the line at the bottom of the page.

Title: **"My Scratch Box"**

Purpose. To provide students with a tactile approach to writing.

Activity: Individual.

Materials: Top of a shoe box with the bottom covered with sand. One for each pupil.

Procedures: Have each child begin to make the initial strokes, up and down, plus circles in the sand. When the letters are introduced on the board, have the students begin to make the letters in the sand. This way they can scratch out the letter and begin again. When they have mastered that, let them begin on paper.

Title **"Skill Sheets"**

Purpose. The student will develop his skill in manuscript writing by using skill sheets.

Activity: Individualized instruction.

Materials: The teacher should provide the child with a transparency folder in which the letters of the alphabet are enclosed. The child can write on top of the transparency with a grease pencil and never touch the paper with the letters written on it. The folder is two sheets of transparency taped together at one of the smaller sides: The inside sheets can be slipped in and out and changed easily.

Procedure: Give the child the folder and have the letters written correctly so he can trace over them and learn the correct formation of the letter. On the rest of the line, the child then has room to practice the letter formation.

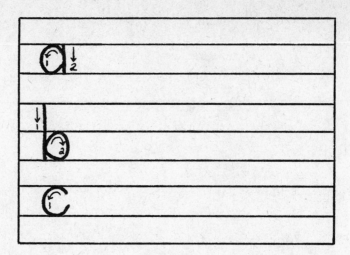

Title:	**"Making Calendars"**
Purpose:	To provide practice in writing numerals.
Activity:	Independent.
Materials:	The instructor passes out a mimeographed copy of a blank calendar with room at the top for a picture. The children are given pencils and assorted crayons, along with a copy of the blank calendar. A large calendar for the month is displayed.
Procedure:	The class is instructed to fill in the blank calendar with the correct numerals using the calendar in front of the room as a guide. They also fill in the month and the names of the days. (The teacher writes these on the

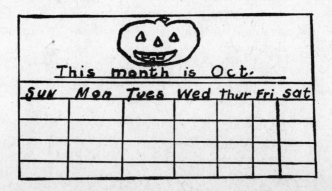

board.) The students may then draw and color a picture at the top of the paper. Calendars can be displayed.

Title: **"Frame It"**

Purpose: To stimulate the students to do their best in cursive writing.

Activity: Independent.

Materials: A very elaborate handmade frame. A box containing slips of paper on which are written interesting subjects.

Procedure: Each week, a student is to pick a folded slip of paper from a box. The paper will have an interesting subject on it. He is to write a sentence about the subject in his very best cursive writing. The student is given time, assistance, and praise as he writes his sentence. The teacher checks the paper and makes sure it is done as well as possible. The student's paper is to be placed in the frame for the week.

Title: **"Cursive Introduction"**

Purpose: To introduce cursive handwriting; to create a desire to write well in both manuscript and cursive; to distinguish between cursive and manuscript writing.

Activity: Independent.

Materials: Christmas stocking, pine scent, enlarged letter to Santa Claus, individual dittoed work sheets

Procedure:
1. Have students close eyes and spray pine scent about the room.
2. Have students guess what the smell is and what it reminds them of.
3. Pass stocking around to each child and discuss what goes in it.
4. Ask how we contact Santa Claus. By telephone? By telegraph?
5. Show enlarged letter to Santa Claus. (Could be a transparency on the overhead projector.)

6. Ask if any students have ever seen this kind of writing before and where.
7. Ask if anyone if familiar with term for "real writing." Write it on the board in Cursive and Manuscript.
8. Discuss what cursive means.
9. Note differences in cursive and manuscript-slant, letters and where we begin letters.
10. Have them read letter or alphabet they recognize.
11. Pass out practice sheets and show undercurve stroke.
12. Have children practice on their sheets.

Title:	**"Finish Writing"**
Purpose:	To teach children how to form letters either manuscript or cursive.
Activity:	Group.
Materials:	Blackboard and chalk.
Procedure:	Teacher makes a symbol on the board (a circle). The student must write on his paper all the letters that he makes starting with the certain stroke. This can also be used with cursive writing.

Teacher draws ◯ on the board. ⟳ She
demonstrates which way she drew it.
The students then draw on their papers the
following letters:

       a   d   o   g   q

The next stroke might be ⇃⇂. Students would
make the following letters:

       b   h   k   l

Title:	**"Letter-O"**
Purpose:	To help correctly form lower and upper case cursive letters and to distinguish between upper and lower case cursive letters.
Activity:	Group.
Materials:	Letter-O cards with upper and lower case letters written on them

Procedure:	1. Group your poor handwriting students to play Letter-O.
	2. Give each student a Letter-O card.

3. Have the group pick one person to call out the letters on the small cards.

4. When the small letter card is called, the student with the letter on his Letter-O card traces over the letter on his card.

5. The first student to get a row of letters up, down, or across then becomes the card caller.

Title:	**"Handwriting Technicalities"**
Purpose:	To enable students to practice and evaluate their handwriting and to see the value of good handwriting.
Activity:	Independent and group.
Materials:	Ditto copies for each child with various sentences demonstrating writing errors to be corrected.
Procedure:	The instructor may begin this lesson by writing a few sentences on the board in which mistakes in letter size, form, spacing, and relative heights have been made. Discuss these problems and give each student the ditto sheet with these errors and have him rewrite the sentences as he thinks they should be.

I wish I could play ball better.

The boys all went out to play.

They all left to go to the store.

Title:	**"Letter C"**
Purpose:	To teach slow students how to write the letter C.
Activity:	Group.
Materials:	Picture file of cats, cars, cans, and cows. Ditto of alphabet, cat and numbers.

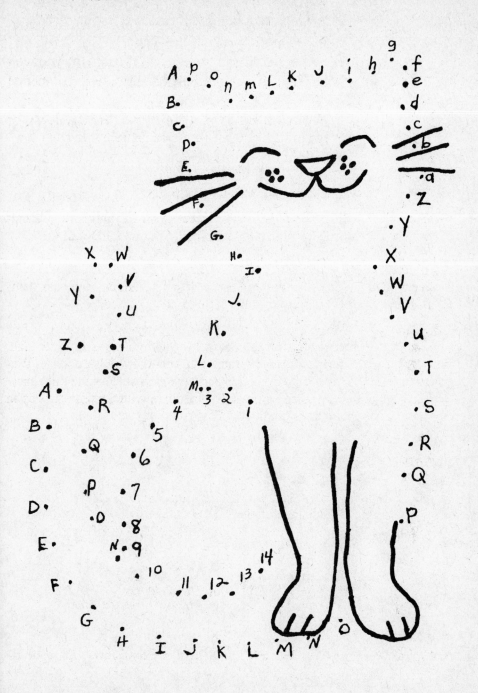

Procedure: 1. Pass out ditto sheets as illustrated.

2. Give directions; only names go on the pages; wait for further directions.

3. Say find #1 and continue to draw a line connecting each number to #14.

4. Place your left hand on top of the paper, and locate the letter A. Draw a line through the alphabet letters.

5. Ask students to identify the object. (Cat) What letter did we make? (C)

6. Emphasize the stroke and formation of the letter C.

7. Students write the letter C five (5) times.

8. Students identify words that begin with the letter C

9. Students write each of these words.

10. Students circle their best handwriting.

Title.   **"Riddles"**

Purpose: To provide interesting handwriting practice.

Activity: Individual or group.

Materials: Pencils, writing paper, and crayons.

Procedure: The teacher will draw a picture of an object on the board

FRONT

I am green.
I wear a star.
I have many
presents

BACK

I wear a big bow.
I'm covered with
  bright paper.
I am a surprise!

and under it write a riddle about it for a "clue." The children will choose the correct answer from a list on the board. Then the class can draw their own illustrations and color them. There should be room on each paper for four riddles. The theme can be changed to suit the seasons or a particular holiday.

Title:	**"I Am"**
Purpose:	To provide interesting writing practice.
Activity:	Independent or group.
Materials:	Piece of white unlined paper for each child.
Procedure:	After the children have spent several days on lines and circles, their names, and single words, the teacher starts practicing the alphabet again. She then lets them write a sentence such as "I am a boy," if he is and "I am a

girl,'' if she is. Pass a piece of unlined paper to each child. Ask them to fold the paper in half lengthwise, and then fold the bottom half to the center line. Then fold it again. This provides folded lines to follow. Tell the children to practice the letters a, b, i, m, o, g, I, R, L, y, then tell them to write the sentence on one of the bottom folds and then draw a picture in the top half to illustrate their sentences.

Title:	**"Alphabet Fish"**
Purpose:	To give concrete experience with the shapes of the manuscript letters of the alphabet. To reinforce the formation of letters, and for practice.
Activity:	Group.
Materials:	Flannelboard, felt shapes, "fishing" pole with magnet, paper fish with paper clip taped to underside.
Procedure:	Introduce subject matter. Have student "fish" for letter. Make letter shape of "fish" caught on flannelboard. Direct everyone in class to write the letter as the pupil writes the letter on the board.

Title:	**"Cursive Writing Championship"**
Purpose:	To motivate a desire to improve handwriting skills.
Activity:	Group.

Materials: Paper, pens or pencils, blue, red, yellow ribbons.

Procedure: 1. After several months of practicing handwriting, hold a contest for 1st, 2nd, and 3rd place in handwriting.

2. Have class nominate several people for judges and vote for five.

3. Everyone should submit a page of handwriting of an agreed-upon paragraph.

4. Each page will be numbered, with only the teacher having the sheet of corresponding names.

5. The handwriting samples should be placed around the room in art gallery style.

6. Each student should be given tokens to place beneath the sample they think is best.

7. The samples that receive eight or more tokens will be evaluated by the judges to determine the winners.

A variation would be to evaluate those who have made the greatest progress. A comparison of present efforts with beginning handwriting samples could be used.

Title: **"Self-Description"**

Purpose: To motivate children to develop legible handwriting.

Activity: Group.

Materials: Writing paper, pens, pencils.

Procedure: Teacher passes out sheets of paper. She tells class to write as fast as they can a description of what they are wearing. The time is set at one minute. No names are to be written on the paper. All the papers are collected. The teacher calls a student to pick a paper and read it to the class. All try to guess who it is. If handwriting is not legible, then another paper is selected. When a few papers that cannot be read have been selected, the teacher points out the importance of writing legibility.

Example: I have a red shirt. I have a green sweater.

Title: **"Poetry and Handwriting"**

Purpose: To encourage and improve the child's handwriting and to encourage the child to be creative in thinking.

Activity: Group.

Materials: A poem, paper and pencils, crayons, yarn, and colored construction paper.

Procedure: Select a short poem according to the season, weather, etc., that reviews the letters of the alphabet, and write it on the board. Then go over any problem letters. Next, let the class copy the poem off the board in their best manuscript form. After each child finishes, let him draw a picture at the bottom of his paper explaining what he thinks the poem is about.

A poem like this could be done periodically and a notebook kept of the poems and drawings. Colored construction paper could be used for the cover and back and tied with yarn. Each child would then have his own book of poetry and illustrations in his own best handwriting.

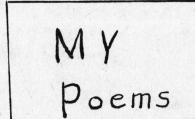

Title: **"Relaxing Writing"**

Purpose: To stress proper positional techniques in preparing class for a handwriting lesson.

Activity: Group.

Materials: Tape recorder.

Procedure: Make a tape recording to prepare class for handwriting lesson. This will be helpful if teacher is putting lines on the board or handing out writing papers. The tape could be in poetry or musical form, as:

"One, two; we're ready to write; are you?
Three, four; put your feet flat on the floor.
Five, six; pick up your magic sticks.
Seven, eight; sit up nice and straight.
Nine, ten; are you now ready to begin?"

Title: **"Using Clichés for Alignment Practice"**

Purpose: To stress alignment while also learning about clichés.

Activity: Group.

Procedure: Explain that a cliché is a trite and over-used phrase that is best avoided. Put a list of such terms on the board and have the students make sentences using more imaginative phrases or words in the cliché's place. Have students think of others. Stress writing alignment when that is important. You can stress spacing, proportion and letter form, too.

Examples: "Busy as a cat on a hot tin roof"

"Raining cats and dogs"

"Silly as a goose"

"Saving for a rainy day"

"Left holding the bag"

Title. **"Mouse Mystery"**

Purpose: To provide interesting handwriting lesson, and practice on selected letters.

Activity: Group.

Materials: Ditto sheet hand-outs.

Procedure: Teacher passes out ditto sheets to children during handwriting lesson and introduces the Mouse Mystery to the children. "Let's all be detectives and find the missing letters. Once we find them, write them carefully in the blanks provided, and once you have completed the hand out, we will go over them and see what good detectives we've been."

WRITE THE MISSING LETTERS.

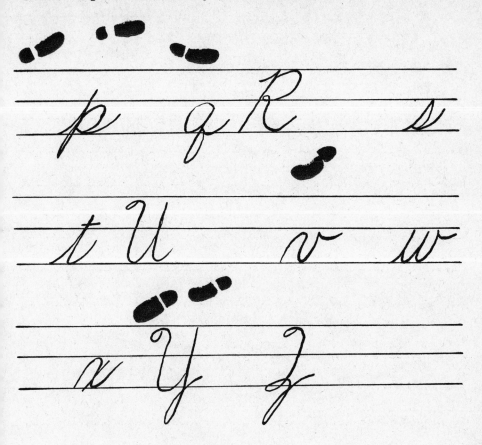

Title:	**"Copying Poems"**
Purpose:	To provide handwriting drill on size, alignment, and spacing.
Activity:	Group or individual.
Materials:	Poems brought by students.
Procedure:	Let students bring to class a poem of their choice. (Good for holiday use.) Have the students copy their poems using their best handwriting . . . remembering to pay close attention to size of letters, alignment and spacing of

letters and words. DO NOT RUSH THEM! Make a bulletin board displaying the papers.

Title: **"Crayon Pictures"**

Purpose: To provide practice in making circles and lines from left to right as readiness for manuscript writing.

Activity: Pre-writing for group.

Materials: Newsprint paper, one dark crayon per child.

Procedure: The teacher makes an illustration step by step on the chalkboard. Child does the same on his paper. Teacher chooses a child to tell what he thinks each finished illustration looks like. If the child's paper is folded to make lines, and the child follows the teacher's lead in making the illustrations, he is also learning to proceed left to right. These are not all used at one sitting.

CHAPTER 5

Teaching Correct Usage

in Written Language:

26 Classroom Activities

The teaching of correct word usage, punctuation, and sentence sense, has been challenging to all teachers, to say the least, frustrating to be sure, and in all probability boring much of the time because drill is the usual mode of operation. Help is provided in this chapter, for here are many interesting activities to enliven your usage instruction.

Knowing when to use would and will, sit and set, there and they're, a period or a question mark are usage elements school children frequently find difficult to learn. Although drill and seat work exercises are tried and true valuable strategies, interesting activities such as the ones contained in this chapter will not only relieve the tedium of the usual classroom fare, but will facilitate the learning your students need to acquire relative to correct usage.

To begin with, there are independent learning activities children can pursue on their own. Following these are games and group activities for small-or large-group learning situations, permitting you the opportunity to individualize your program. While some children are participating in a group activity, others may be working alone or playing a game. Versatility is your option.

Title: **"Halting the Word Traffic"**

Purpose: To provide practice placing a period at the end of declarative sentences.

Activity: Independent.

Materials: Copies of a short story written in simple declarative sentences. Exclude all periods from the story, and "decorate" the story by placing a stoplight after each word and a line with wheels on it under each word, so each word will look like a vehicle. Also, stencils with all the stoplights to be colored red, punched out.

Procedure: Pass out materials. Tell the class they are going to be traffic engineers, and straighten out a traffic jam of words. To straighten it out, they should color the stoplights red where a period should be. They may color the other traffic lights green if they like. After they have finished, they may come to your desk and get a stencil to place over their own paper to check it.

Once upon a time there was a green wiggly fish his best friend was a black snake

Title: **"Sentence Building"**

Purpose: To give the student the opportunity to build sentences with a variety of subjects, verbs, and modifiers.

Activity: Independent.

Procedure: Divide a spiral notebook into three sections. In the first section put various subjects, verbs in the second section, and modifiers in the third section.

Let the child build sentences using the different sections, and make sure that the sentences make good sense.

The bird	ran	slowly.
A cat	swim	heavily.
That man	flew	swiftly.
Many fish	breathes	quietly.

Subject #1 could be paired with verb #3 and modifiers #1, #3, or #4.

Subject #2 could be matched with verb #1 or #4 and modifiers #1, #2, #3, or #4.

Title:	**"Creepy Contractions"**
Purpose:	To help students in using contractions—how to form a contraction, what they mean, use in sentences.
Activity:	Independent. Useful for either class work or a test.
Materials:	Posters showing a witch, bat, cat, and a ghost. Each object has specific words on it. One Creepy Contraction question sheet per student.
Procedure:	Pass out ditto sheets to students. Students read questions and answer by referring to the posters.

CREEPY CONTRACTIONS

1. Look at the witch's broom. Write a contraction using this word. _____

poster

2. On the ghost is a contraction that means you are. Can you find the contraction? _____

3. Find a contraction on the cat that means the same as two words in the sentence below. (Write it below the two words.)

    Do not be afraid of the cat.

4. Look at the ghost. Find the contraction *won't*. What does it mean? _____

5. What is wrong with the word on the bat?
    _____

6. The contraction on the witch hat means
    _____

7. Which contraction on the ghost means did not?
    _____

8. Look at the cat's tail. Use this word to form two contractions. _____

9. Write a contraction that means the same as the words on the witch's dress. _____

10. Find a contraction on the ghost to fill in this sentence.

    _____ run away from the ghost. What does this contraction mean?

Title: **"A Grammatical Autobiography"**

Purpose: To help students learn grammatical usage terms in relation to their personal experiences.

Activity: Independent.

Procedure: Assign a grammatical usage term to be used in meaningful context.

Illustration: List ten ambitions in infinitive phrases.

Write eight or ten sentences about your personality, each beginning with a prepositional phrase.

Describe your family, using adjectives but not adverbs.

Title: **"The "Why" of Parts of Speech"**

Purpose: To help students understand the functional value of the different parts of speech.

Activity: Independent or group.

Materials: Examples of parts of speech

Procedure: Have the students try to write a story, using only nouns and verbs. This will point up the importance of other speech parts—adverbs, and adjectives, prepositions, conjunctions, interjections, and pronouns—which often suffer gross subordination to nouns and verbs.

Illustration: John ran. Susie skipped. Rover eats bones.

Title: **"Sentence Fun"**

Purpose: To develop ability to recognize sentences as opposed to sentence fragments.

Activity: Independent.

Materials: Ditto practice sheet.

Procedure: The pupils match a group of sentence fragments like the following.

Directions: On the line to the left of each group of words in the first column, write the number of the group of words in the second column that finishes the sentences.

| Stephen had found | 1. a broken leg. |
| The crow had | 2. Stephen's pet. |

Stephen took	3. a crow.
The crow became	4. the crow home with him.
The dog	5. going to my aunt's.
I am	6. ran very fast.
Little Red Hen	7. was tired.
After much play, Jack	8. baked some bread.
The little dog	9. the zoo.
Jimmy visited	10. barked at the stranger.

Title: **"Catch the Error"**

Purpose: To aid the student in identifying and correcting grammatical errors.

Activity: Independent or group.

Materials: Tape recorder—Tape of a story with grammatical errors.

Procedure: Have the students listen to a tape of a story with 20 grammatical errors, told slowly. The students are to count and list them. The errors should be so spaced on the tape that the student has time to write them down. Play the tape back and let selected students identify the errors.

Title: **"Standard Usage"**

Purpose: Students will learn to identify the colloquial term in context, substitute the standard term, and compose original sentences using the standard term.

Activity: Game.

Materials: Sentences containing colloquial terms. Cards with sentences which may or may not contain colloquial terms. Tape recorder.

Procedure: Put sentences that contain colloquial terms on the chalkboard. Have students suggest the colloquial terms and possible standard terms. After establishing the colloquial and standard term in each sentence, group the students into teams. One team will read a sentence from a teacher-prepared card which may or may not contain a colloquial term. The opposite team will try to find the error and correct it. To allow the students opportunity to use the standard terms, have role play as news reporters. The news report will be composed one sentence at a time with a different student contributing a sentence containing one of the standard terms learned in the lesson.

Illustration: SENTENCES

1. Try and come early.
2. He sat in back of us.
3. He left at about noon.
4. They blame it on us.
5. Return inside of a week.
6. No one outside of Al slept.

COLLOQUIAL	STANDARD
1. try and	try to
2. in back of	behind
3. at (or about)	at (or about)
4. blamed it on	blamed
5. inside of	within
6. outside of	except

Title: **"Let's Race"**

Purpose: To provide practice in correct usage of words that are often mispronounced.

Activity: Game.

Materials: Flannelboard or chalkboard, stick-on cars. Sentences listed on separate sheets of paper.

The sentences will include words that are often mispronounced, i.e., can go (kin go) what will (wha'll).

Procedure: Class is divided into three teams with three drivers. The driver picks a piece of paper and calls on someone from his team to give the correct sentence. If they get it correct, they move their car forward a square. If they get it wrong, they move back a square. First team to finish wins the race.

START   FINISH

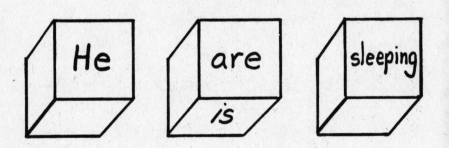

Title: **"Am I Correct?"**

Purpose: As a reinforcement for teaching use of the verbs *is*, *am*, and *are*.

Activity: Game.

Materials: Blocks, colored paper, and masking tape. Paper can be changed to keep interest.

Procedure: Children roll the blocks. If the sentence comes up correct and the child can say that it is correct, he gets 3 points. If it is incorrect, he is allowed to change the verb block to the correct word. If he does so correctly, he gets 5 points.

Title: **"Letter Format"**

Purpose: To review the correct writing of letters and the addressing of envelopes.

Activity: Group.

Materials: 6″ x 8″ file cards; whole and cut into strips

Procedure: Each card has separate parts of a letter. Individual stu-
                 dents place them in the correct order on the chalkboard.
                 Large card (representing the envelope) is placed on board
                 and strips placed in the correct positions.

Variation: Can be played as team game.

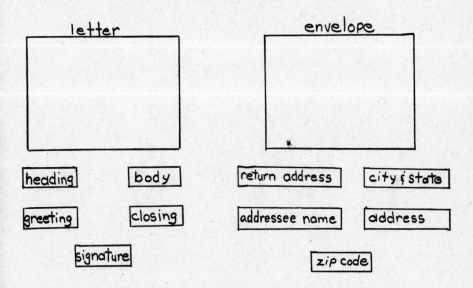

Title: **"Subjects and Predicates"**

Purpose: The purpose of this teaching idea is to aid the student to
                 recognize the subject and predicate in a sentence.

Activity: Group

Procedure: The teacher should draw two replicas of houses on the
                 board (or make a ditto with two drawings of houses). One
                 house should be entitled "SUBJECT" and the other
                 should be entitled "PREDICATE". Then the teacher
                 should write a list of sentences.

                 After the stage is set, the teacher asks the students to see
                 if they can help the "who or what" words and the "what

they did or what happened" words find their way home. The teacher points to the houses "SUBJECT" and "PREDICATE". The student should know or be instructed to know before playing this game that the word "subject" is synonymous with *who* or *what* and that the word "predicate" is synonymous with *what they did* or *what happened*. Then the student should choose the appropriate words from the sentences that go with their respective houses. As the student chooses a correct one, he should be called to the board to write his choice in the appropriate house. Then, more students are called upon until the list is gone and the houses are filled with inhabitants (subjects and predicates).

The turkey is fat.

Many Pilgrims came to the New World.

The Indians were friendly to the Pilgrims.

Thanksgiving is a festive holiday.

We eat turkey and dressing on Thanksgiving.

The family is ready to eat.

(The sentences could be composed to coordinate with the time of the year, holidays, or subjects that the students are studying.)

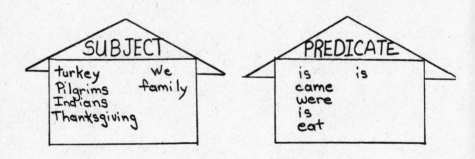

Title:	**"Usage of: Can, May, Sit, and Set"**
Purpose:	To help children learn the correct usage of *can* and *may*; *sit* and *set*.
Activity:	Group.

Materials: Six posters or transparencies (use both sides of three posters). Use one poster each to illustrate in sentences the correct usage of *can* and *may*, *sit* and *set*. On the other posters, have blanks in sentences to be filled in with *can* and *may* on one, *sit and set* on other.

Procedure: For each verb, show the class a poster with correct sentences using the verb. Ask them to make up a rule for the usage of the verb. Show them sentences using *can* and *may*, and then have blanks in sentences for the class to respond to orally, and fill in either *can* or *may*. Do the same for *sit* and *set*.

Title: **"Similes"**

Purpose: To acquaint students with similes, and motivate application through creative writing.

Activity: Group.

Materials: Poem, "As"; paper and pencil

Procedure: Give the students the poem, "As." You want them to discover and tell you what they observe about the poem: rhyming couplets, contrast between first and second half of each line, mental pictures can be made, etc. Discuss the word, *simile*, with the students and allow them to suggest some new similes. To begin you may give them part of a simile. For example, as light as a   ; as heavy as a   ; as   as a turtle. Encourage them to use exciting adjectives such as *courageous, tantalizing*, and *bland*. Challenge the students to write their own poem of similes.

AS

As wet as a fish—as dry as a bone;
As live as a bird—as dead as a stone;
As plump as a partridge—as poor as a rat;
As strong as a horse—as weak as a cat;
As hard as a flint—as soft as a mole;
As white as a lily—as black as a coal;

As heavy as lead—as light as a feather;
As steady as time—as uncertain as weather;
As flat as a flounder—as round as a ball;
As blunt as a hammer—as sharp as an awl;
As brittle as glass—as tough as gristle;
As neat as a pin—as clean as a whistle;
As red as a rose—as square as a box;
As bold as a thief—as sly as a fox.

—Anonymous

Title:	**"Ghost Story"**
Purpose:	To assess and correct oral and written grammatical usage.
Activity:	Group.
Materials:	Tape recorder.
Procedure:	Have everyone sit in a circle if possible. Teacher will start a ghost story. Everyone around the room will take his turn at continuing the story. Next, listen to the replay for grammar mistakes. Write them down in the correct form on chalkboard. Next, ask students to write their own ghost story. Then let them work in pairs to correct grammar, misspelled words and punctuation. Then after stories are written in correct form—collect and make a book—read all stories without the author's name. Ask students to write title of story and who they think the author of the story might be. Ask the one who wins to add his paper to the front of the book for the Table of Contents.

Title:	**"Traffic Light"**
Purpose:	To increase awareness of, and skill in, obeying the signals given by the comma, period, question mark, and exclamation point.
Activity:	Group.

Materials: Traffic light made from construction paper.

Procedure: Tack traffic light up near reading table. After each student reads a short selection, and how many times he had to pause for the caution signal (,), or stop for the stop signals (. ! ?). Use as a teaching aid to remind students when they are overlooking these signs. Explain that obeying these signals makes it easier to understand what the author intended for us to read and that in writing we use punctuation marks as signals to the reader enabling him to understand what he reads.

Title: **"Finding the Punctuation"**

Purpose: To help develop oral punctuation in oral reading.

Activity: Group.

Materials: Tape recorder, paper, pens.

Procedure: Have óne child write a few sentences using as many different types of punctuation as possible. Have him record them on tape the way they are written. Have a second child listen to the tape and write the sentences down using the punctuation he hears. Have the two children look at both papers and discuss the good and bad points.

Title:	**"Adding Color to Written Expression"**
Purpose:	To teach the value of good verbs.
Activity:	Group.
Materials:	Chalkboard or overhead projector.
Procedure:	Write the following statement on the board or overhead projector:

"He went down the street."

Ask the class to change the verb *went* to a more colorful word. After they have listed theirs, write these:

vanished   whirled   limped   streaked   trembled
whipped   hobbled   ripped   stamped   shook

Try these words out in the verb slot in the sentence. Call on students to point out how much more each colorful verb tells about the way the man went down the street. Once you have inspired children to use good verbs, help them remember ones they know and encourage them to use new ones. Write another verb on the board, and this time have the pupils provide the substitutions.

Title:	**"Sentence Strips"**
Purpose:	To teach sentence structure.
Activity:	Group.
Procedure:	Make up sentences which can be inverted either to make a question or a statement, such as "The boys can play." "Can the boys play?"

Write the words on 1″ x 5″ strips of paper and join the ends with brass fasteners. Have the children manipulate the strips of paper to make a telling and then an asking sentence.

```
┌──┬───────┬──┬───────┬──┬───────┬──────────┬──┐
│○ │  Can  │○○│  the  │○ │ boys  │○○│  play  │○ │
│○ │       │○○│       │○ │       │○○│        │○ │
└──┴───────┴──┴───────┴──┴───────┴──────────┴──┘

┌──┬───────┬──┬───────┬──┬───────┬──────────┬──┐
│○ │  The  │○ │ boys  │○ │  can  │○ │  play  │○ │
│○ │       │○ │       │○ │       │○ │        │○ │
└──┴───────┴──┴───────┴──┴───────┴──────────┴──┘

┌──┬──────┬──┬─────┬──┬──────┬──┬──────┬──┬────┬──┬─────┬──┬──────────┬──┐
│○ │ The  │○ │ sun │○ │ will │○ │ rise │○ │ in │○ │ the │○ │ morning  │○ │
│○ │      │○ │     │○ │      │○ │      │○ │    │○ │     │○ │          │○ │
└──┴──────┴──┴─────┴──┴──────┴──┴──────┴──┴────┴──┴─────┴──┴──────────┴──┘

┌──┬──────┬──┬─────┬──┬─────┬──┬──────┬──┬────┬──┬─────┬──┬──────────┬──┐
│○ │ Will │○ │ the │○ │ sun │○ │ rise │○ │ in │○ │ the │○ │ morning  │○ │
│○ │      │○ │     │○ │     │○ │      │○ │    │○ │     │○ │          │○ │
└──┴──────┴──┴─────┴──┴─────┴──┴──────┴──┴────┴──┴─────┴──┴──────────┴──┘
```

Title:	**"Finding a Complete Sentence"**
Purpose:	To develop students' ability to identify a complete sentence.
Activity:	Group.
Materials:	Magazines, scissors.
Procedure:	Magazines are a source for this activity. The teacher should go through and find examples of complete sentences, incomplete sentences, runons, fragments, improper punctuation, improper use of vocabulary and any others you see. Students can identify many of the advertising slogans from magazines because they have seen them used so much on television. Have the students identify what kind of a sentence they see when you show a particular slogan. Then have groups of students go through magazines and find their own examples of types of sentence structure. If they see errors of capitalization, punctuation, or syllabication then they are to cut them out for discussion. This activity helps students to evaluate and become critical readers.
Illustration:	Always room for Jell-O.
	(An incomplete sentence (fragment). Jello is divided into syllables in the wrong place.)

Title:	**Choose a Verb.**
Purpose:	To provide a stimulating way of writing a sentence with correct verb usage.

Activity: Group.

Materials: Overhead projector and marker.

Procedure: Tell the students the purpose of the activity is to write a sentence correctly. Give them two frequently misused verbs. *May* and *can* would be good verbs for this activity. The teacher chooses a student and he thinks of a sentence using *may* or *can*. He writes the first word of the sentence on the overhead projector. The next student looks at that word and thinks of a sentence. He must use the first word written on the overhead, and add his word. This continues until the sentence is completed. The students must keep in mind that only the verbs given by the teacher may be used. If the sentence does not make sense as a student adds a word, he must tell the sentence he has in mind.

Example:
1st. student: I

2nd. student: I can

3rd. student: I can run.

Title: **"Puny Punctuation"**

Purpose: To develop skill in punctuation and sentence sense.

Activity: Group.

Materials: Examples of sentences that can be changed in meaning by changing the punctuation.

Procedure: Teacher dictates a sentence using different punctuation. Students write the sentence and punctuate it as they think it should be. Then the teacher dictates the same sentence using different punctuation; again students write sentence with correct punctuation. Compare the two sentences, pointing out the different meaning caused by different punctuation.

Ask students to write their own sentences. Give each one a turn to read his sentence aloud as the teacher did.

Illustration: Woman without her man is nothing. Woman! Without her, man is nothing.

Title:	**"Fill in the Blank"**
Purpose:	To increase correct homonym usage skills.
Activity:	Group.
Materials:	Dittos with a story with deleted words.
Procedure:	When studying words which have similar sounds but are spelled differently, supply class with dittos. Each child selects a partner; one reads, the other writes the answers using such words as TO, TOO, TWO. Start the groups with these hints (to—toward), (too—also), and (two——number).
	Read the story aloud for the class.
Illustration:	Timothy Bunny sniffed. Something smelled good. He hopped quietly over _____ the window and peeked out. There, on the lawn, he saw his ____ sisters and _____ brothers. He could hear them giggling. He heard Sue say, "Oh, that's _____ funny."

Title:	**"Guess the Word"**
Purpose:	To help the child more fully recognize parts of speech.
Activity:	Group.
Procedure:	Divide the group into two teams. Write a sentence on the blackboard. A child is chosen to select a word from the sentence, but does not tell the class. Each student may ask two questions about the secretly chosen word. If a child gets the word correct on the first question, then five points are given to his team, but if he gets it on the second question, then the team gets two points.
Illustration:	Sentence:
	The *little* boy came running into the house with a ten-dollar bill that he found on the muddy street.
	Question: Is the word an adverb?
	Answer: No, it is not an adverb.
	Question: Is the word an adjective?
	Answer: Yes, the word is an adjective.
	Question: Is the word 'muddy'.

Answer: No.

Then go to another player.

Title:	**"Signals for Sentences"**
Purpose:	To aid children in learning punctuation.
Activity:	Group.
Materials:	Traffic signals made out of construction paper.
Procedure:	Hold up traffic signals and ask children how they can relate these to punctuation marks. The traffic signals could stand for the following punctuation marks.

        Stop sign—period
        Yield sign—comma
        Caution sign—exclamation point
        Information sign—question mark

Then have the children write a couple of sentences without any punctuation marks. Collect the sentences and have a child read them out loud. Then have children take turns punctuating them.

Title:	**"The Wheel Game"**
Purpose:	To teach the mechanics of written communication, the purpose of punctuation.
Activity:	Independent.
Materials:	Three disks and a brad: first one 10″ second one 8″ third one 1½″

Procedure: Write the first part of a sentence of the largest circle, the second part of the sentence on the middle circle, and the punctuation on the smallest circle.

Have the child work the wheel and see what difference punctuation makes to the sentence.

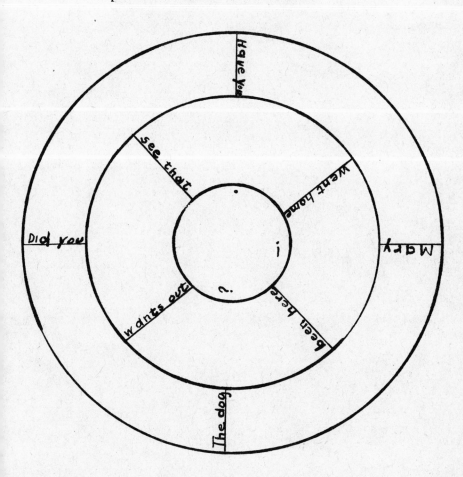

CHAPTER 6

Sparking Written Expression with

37 Classroom Activities

Developing students' written expression skills is a difficult task demanding much imagination on the part of teachers. It requires a two-fold thrust of improving technical skills such as sentence sequence, paragraphing, etc., and stimulating creative writing abilities. While you have probably developed many of your own excellent instructional strategies to meet these goals, you will be able to supplement and complement them with the 37 written expression activities found in this chapter.

There are times when group learning activities are not only economical of the teacher's stamina but more productive than individual assignments. Yet, independent activities are indispensable and must be a part of the instructional program. To help your grouping strategy, whether group or individual or a combination of the two, the written expression learning activities are divided and arranged for your convenience. The first part of the chapter contains independent learning activities, and the latter, group activities.

Although you may want to use one idea at a time, especially when first starting, the availability of activities for both independent and group situations provides you with much flexibility. For example, you could be using a group activity to instruct several children together, and in the same time frame, other students could be doing independent activities appropriate for their individual needs.

Creative writing development is not only desirable but necessary in any language arts program. Many activities in this chapter will give an assist and a lift to your instructional efforts. But also included are activities pertaining to fundamental written expression skills. "Oral Sentence Building" is an activity for facilitating skill in sentence development while "What Happened" helps students write descriptive paragraphs. To teach children correct form, "Personal Letters" is available, and other activities stimulate story sequence and sequencing paragraphs. With this array, you will have increased your capability to provide sufficient writing opportunities that will help your students to overcome anemic skills in this important language art.

Title:	**"Want Ads"**
Purpose:	To give students a chance to design and make a classified ad.
Activity:	Independent.
Materials:	Newspaper, pencil, paper.
Procedure:	Ask the children to bring in a previous day's newspaper. Each should have a copy of the same edition. Suggest to the class that they look at the advertisements in the classified section and examine them closely. Let each student pretend he is going to sell some object he owns and design a classified ad to put in the class paper.

Title:	**"Shipwrecked"**
Purpose:	To develop creative writing abilities and imaginations.
Activity:	Independent.
Materials:	Paper and pencil.
Procedure:	This activity can be scheduled for as long as you feel necessary. To help students use their imaginations in constructing a diary, first, tell them to imagine they are aboard a ship somewhere in the Atlantic Ocean. Suddenly, the ship is rocked by a terrible explosion! Struggling, you manage to swim to an empty life raft as the ship sinks beneath the waves. Several days later you are washed ashore on an island. The island seems deserted.

In your diary, tell about life on the island. Keep a day-to-day account of what happens. After diaries are made, suggest that from this source material they can create imaginative stories.

Title:	**"Fractured Fairy Tales"**
Purpose:	To develop creative written expression.
Activity:	Independent.
Materials:	Book of fairy tales, paper, and pencil.
Procedure:	Read a fairy tale to the class. Let the children discuss ideas of how to make the tale a modern version. Then write the new version on the board. After the discussion, read the new version to them. After this group effort, let the children create their own versions of other fairy tales. For those who wish to read their stories to the class, allow time. This reward will further their motivation the next time.

Title:	**"Creative Writing Forms Creative Art"**
Purpose:	To provide motivation for creative writing.
Activity:	Independent or group.
Materials:	Art supplies.
Procedure:	Let the students paint a picture about a very memorable event (vacation, last weekend, at the Fair, etc.). Display all pictures.
	Next day: Talk about pictures and what they might suggest to *different* individuals. Then have students select *any* one of the pictures displayed (his own or another), and write a story about it. Let them work in pairs to give suggestions and proofread, if they prefer.
	Next day: Let volunteers read their story; then display it below the picture they chose to write about.
	When all are displayed, discuss the picture which attracted the most stories.

Title:	**"Dear Mike"**
Purpose:	Using a letter to motivate writing.
Activity:	Independent.
Procedure:	Write the following letter on the chalkboard or duplicate it so each child can have a copy.

Dear Mike,

    I hesitated a long time before writing you this letter, for I know you've suffered a great shock. I just want you to know that my offer still stands. Please call me soon to tell me of your plans.

Paul

The students can discuss the identities of Mike and Paul. Why was the letter written? What is the shock to which Paul refers? Each student can write a story about these two characters.

Title:	**"Animal Crackers"**
Purpose:	Creative writing.
Activity:	Independent.
Materials:	One or two boxes of animal crackers. Paper and pencil.
Procedure:	Each child is given an animal cracker. He answers questions about the animal to write a story.

Is the animal imaginary?
What does it eat?
Where does it live?
What can it see, hear?
How does it feel, smell?
Does it make sounds?

Then he eats the animal cracker.

Title:	**"A Busload of Children"**
Purpose:	To give the students an idea for creative writing and to practice creative expression.
Activity.	Independent.

Materials: A poster with a picture of a bus, (this may be drawn or from a magazine). Also, if you can obtain pictures of children from other countries, add these to the poster.

Procedure: Show the class the poster. Tell them that the bus is filled with children from other countries. Since they came to the United States, all they have been doing is riding the bus. They are grouchy and tired, and so is the bus driver. He doesn't know what they can do that would be fun.

Ask the class if they can think of some things that they enjoy doing that would be fun for the children. After they name a few activities, ask them to write about their favorite activity, or the time they had the most fun so the children on the bus will have ideas of many things to do while they are in the United States.

Title: **"Mystery Boxes"**

Purpose: To motivate children for creative writing.

Activity: Independent.

Materials: Boxes of various sizes and shapes.

Procedure: Say, "Class, I have some boxe: here that are mysterious and magical at the same time. For instance, look at this box. What do you think is inside it? Where did it come from? Who did it belong to? Use your imagination and write a paragraph about one of these boxes."

Illustration: Set boxes of different sizes and shapes on a table for all to see. If enough different types of boxes aren't available, labels can be used. "Captain Blue Beard's Treasure Chest," "Nurses' and Doctors' Kits," "Space Parts," and "Danger! Do Not Open," are but a few suggestions.

Title: **"Observing and Reporting"**

Activity: Group.

Procedure: Three students will enact a brief skit unexpectedly before the class. The class will then be questioned about certain facts concerning the presentation. This is to demonstrate the need to develop skills in observation and accurate reporting.

Skit: 1st Girl—Wearing coat, carries umbrella, rushes into the room, hides umbrella in wastebasket, leaves.

2nd Girl—Wears scarf over head, enters crying, "I must find my purse or mother will be angry!" She finds umbrella, says, "Oh, there it is." (Takes umbrella.)

3rd Girl—Enters, hands the girl something small, unseen, says "You were foolish to give this to (first girl's name) (both leave).

The actors return to their classroom, and now the class will be asked to take paper and pencil so that they can record what happened. Ask questions about the event:

What object was hidden in the wastebasket?
What did the 2nd girl say when she came in the room?
What was the first girl wearing?
What color was the scarf the 2nd girl was wearing?
What did the 3rd girl give to the 2nd girl?
What was the 2nd girl searching for?

It should be interesting to tally the different answers given to see how accurate we really are when we report what we think we see.

Title.   **"Oral Sentence Building"**

Purpose: To teach children to think and write longer, more descriptive, complete sentences.

Activity: Group.

Procedure: Begin with a small sentence.
Example: I can help my mother.
Add an action word.
Example: I can help my mother do her work.
Add a descriptive word.
Example: I can help my mother do her routine work.
Add words to tell where.

> *Example:* I can help my mother do her routine work in the kitchen.
>
> Add words to tell when.
>
> *Example*: I can help my mother do her routine work in the kitchen while she is cooking.
>
> Add words to tell how.
>
> *Example*: I can help my mother do her routine work in the kitchen by setting the table for her while she is cooking.

Title:	**"Creative Writing"**
Purpose:	Creative writing.
Activity:	Group.
Procedure:	In writing poetry, children often have difficulty finding words that rhyme, words that express their feelings, and just the right word to fit in that means what they want to say.

An exercise is shown that will help the children gain practice in finding these right words. This exercise should be tried using a dictionary only as a last resort.

After this exercise is completed, the children should be asked to try and write some type of a poem using some of the words they have found.

In each blank, write a synonym for the word on the left.

sour	tart	___	___	___
odor	___	___	___	___
finish	___	___	___	___
stop	___	___	___	___
speak	___	___	___	___

In each blank write a word that rhymes with the word to the left of it.

door	floor	___	___	___
fail	___	___	___	___
street	___	___	___	___
inch	___	___	___	___
sound	___	___	___	___

In each blank, write a word that expresses the same feeling as the word to the left of it.

mean	selfish	___	___	___
sadness	___	___	___	___
happiness	___	___	___	___
angry	___	___	___	___
love	___	___	___	___

Title: **"Scavenger Hunt"**

Purpose: Writing clear directions.

Activity: Group.

Materials: Envelopes, treasure box with prize inside.

Procedure:
1. Divide into groups of eight.
2. Begin with a message to be given to another group in the room. The message should tell directions for getting to another place in the school from the room. There the second envelope will be found.
3. The teacher will decide according to the group how many envelopes will be placed.
4. Have the treasure at the end—on a shelf, buried in the sand, in the principal's office.
5. All of the children in the chosen group will go together to follow the clues.

Illustration: MESSAGE

1. Turn left at the door.
2. Follow the walk past three trees.
3. Take four giant steps north.
4. Dig for the treasure.

Title: **"Wishing on a Star"**

Purpose: To encourage the children to begin to express themselves creatively and freely in written form.

Activity: Group—Independent.

Materials: Poems on wishing.
                 Ditto with a large star for each child.
                 An example for the children to follow on posterboard.

Procedure: 1. The teacher directs a discussion with the class on wish-
                    ing and ways of wishing.

                 2. The children are asked if they know any poems on
                    wishing; if so, they should be encouraged to share
                    them with the class; if not, the teacher will read, ''The
                    Fairies'' by Rose Fyleman and ''Star Light, Star
                    Bright.'' The latter may be used to let children finish.

                 3. The teacher passes out to each child a ditto with a large
                    star on it having guide lines for writing Each child
                    is instructed to write his own creative expression about

something he is "wishing on his star" and add his name at the bottom.

4. He is then told to cut out his star and color it if he wishes.

5. A wishing bulletin board is made from the class collection.

Title:	**"Greeting-Card Verse"**
Purpose:	To introduce the elements of poetry such as rhythm and meter.
Activity:	Small group or independent.
Materials:	Samples of greeting cards, such as birthday, get-well, anniversary, special occasions, sympathy, etc.
Procedure:	Distribute the sample cards; discuss the different feelings which might be conveyed, such as humor, sadness, joy, sympathy, or concern. This should be conducted in the same manner as a creative writing exercise. Anything should be acceptable and punctuation and capitalization should be accepted as is.

Title:	**"Teleplay"**
Purpose:	To give children an opportunity to write creatively.
Activity:	Group.
Procedure:	Have the children write titles for a story. Then take one of the titles and have one group write a TV script about it. Divide the rest of the class up into several groups and have them write commercials and jingles that could be used. After writing this up, perhaps the class could write invitations to another class and invite them to come and see the play.

Title:	**"Letters for Fun and Fads"**
Purpose:	To help children develop letter-writing skill.
Activity:	Group.
Materials:	Envelopes and post cards.
Procedure:	Directions to Class: If you see something on a cereal box or in a magazine that you would like to send for, I will help you. Here in my desk I'll keep post cards, envelopes, and stamps. You must show me a perfect copy before you can have the post cards, stamps, or envelopes. Let me know when you want to send for something.

KATHY BROWN
ROOM 12
BELLVIEW SCHOOL
BELLVIEW, FL. 32614

Receiving mail is always exciting for all children!!! This meaningful activity will be self-motivating for your students, particularly when they receive replies and can display their own mail.

Title:	**"Writing Group Books"**
Purpose:	To provide creative writing opportunities.
Activity:	Group.
Procedure:	Divide class into *three groups*. These three groups will each produce a book made up of pages contributed by the individual members of the group.

Instruct your students to write a short story about a pet,
an animal they have seen, or one they might like to have.
They are to use one half of the paper for their story, and
the other half for a picture illustrating their story. Each
group can choose a different subject; therefore, there will
be three different books. The papers are collected and
tied together. (Making covers could be a separate activity.)

Title:	**"Hands and Feet Stories"**
Purpose:	To encourage the children to express their thoughts freely in written form.
Activity:	Group.
Materials:	A. Large paper and pencil or pen. B. Clean hands and feet.
Procedure:	Have the children trace around and cut out their two hands and two feet on the paper. While they are doing the above, the teacher places on the chalkboard:

> My hands would like to
> My feet would like to

Tell the children to copy these beginnings on one hand
and one foot and to finish the sentences on the partner for
each, giving them an example to follow on posterboard
or chalkboard.

After they have finished their sentences, have them mount their hands and feet on colored backgrounds. Then let them display their work around the room.

Title:	**"What Happened?"**
Purpose:	To provide practice for students to write descriptive paragraphs describing what has happened sequentially using accurate observations.
Activity:	Group.
Materials:	Costume for the student.
Procedure:	Have one or more students costumed like a robber for example. The costumed student runs into the room and pretends to rob someone using the appropriate dialogue. Then he runs out. The teacher asks students to write down what happened. Ask students to describe the intruder, what he did, what he said, all in the proper sequence. When finished, ask them to write their feelings and reactions to what just happened. Later, after everyone is finished, read some aloud and note any differences. Did everyone see the same thing? This could be done orally, also.

Title:	**"Personal Letters"**
Purpose:	To have students learn correct letter form for friendly letters.

POSTER OR TRANSPARENCY

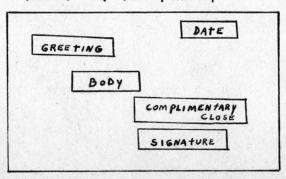

Activity: Group.

Materials: Poster or transparency showing correct letter form.

Procedure: 1. Review of letter parts using poster. Have a student place each part in the correct place. Briefly discuss each part.

                  2. Ask class to write letters to persons of their choice using correct personal letter form.

Title: **"Story Sequence"**

Purpose: To teach paragraph sequence and thought sequence in stories.

Activity: Group.

Materials: Select three stories (more if you like) from a discarded reader. Cut apart each paragraph from all three stories and paste on separate cards. Paste each picture also on a separate cards. The cards should be about as large as one half-page of a reader, so that the half-page illustrations will fit onto the cards. (Cut tagboard for cards.) A box can be used to keep the cards in.

Procedure: Children must first sort out the three stories, deciding which pictures belong to each story. The pictures are placed in horizontal rows. Then the cards showing paragraphs are placed in sequence under the appropriate illustrations, and the completed stories are read.

Title: **"Planning a Trip"**

Purpose: To provide meaningful business letter writing opportunities.

Activity: Group.

Procedure: 1. Tell your students to think of a state they would like to visit.

                  2. The next day have each student write down the name of the state.

                  3. Tell the students that they are to write a letter to the

state capital division of tourism asking for information about some of the attractions and resources of the state. They should state the time of year, mode of travel and particular interests such as camping, historical sights, fishing, etc.

4. When all letters are written and groups have evaluated each member's letter as being correct, all letters should be mailed.

5. As students receive their information, ask them to plan an itinerary of places they would like to visit and the best route to take.

6. Permit volunteers to tell the class or their group their vacation plans.

Title.	**"The Reporters"**
Purpose:	To provide meaningful practice of written expression.
Activity:	Group.
Procedure:	1. Have student choose one thing that has happened during the last week (something that would be interesting to the class and exciting).
	2. After having them read several newspaper articles, have them begin to write about what they saw happen.
	3. When the articles are polished, you could make a ditto of the articles for a class newspaper.

Title:	**"Story Mobiles"**
Purpose:	To provide opportunities for written expression skill development.
Activity:	Group.
Materials:	Hang several articles from a clothes hanger—making a mobile (for example: ribbon, lollipop, pencil, coin purse).
Procedure:	After making your mobile, display it in a conspicuous place in the room. After the children have shown curious-

ity about the collection and asked questions about it, tell them they are to make up a story in which all the objects in the mobile are mentioned.

Title:	**"Painting Colorful Sentences"**
Purpose:	To help students write descriptive sentences colorfully.
Activity:	Group.
Procedure:	Begin with a motivational device showing students several pictures, i.e. color and black and white; a room with very little decoration and one with much decoration. Ask which of the pictures appeal to them. Then show examples of very ordinary sentences such as: The rain fell; The snow is on the tree. Then explain how to expand the sentence to be more colorful. It should be clear that the object is to improve what the sentence says not just to make it longer. Put on the board four or five ordinary sentences and have students improve them by substituting new words, or expanding them.
Examples:	Ordinary: The rain fell. Colorful: A misty rain was falling gently all around the town.

Title:	**"The Five W's"**
Purpose:	To develop skills in descriptive writing.
Activity:	Group.
Materials:	Paper and pencil.
Procedure:	Read an article from a newspaper introducing the five W's: When, Where, Why, Who, and What. Explain how each one of these is used in the article. Let the student try to pick out each W and tell why he chose that. Let the student select a topic that he wishes to write on and make sure he uses the five W's. After he does this, let him read his article aloud and have the other students try to find the W's that are in the article.

Title: **"The Way I See It"**

Purpose: To provide creative writing opportunities.

Activity: Group.

Material: Paper and pencil.

Procedure: Write on the chalkboard several historical events which your class has previously studied. Have slips of paper written with different animals or objects named (one for each person in class). Examples: dog, horse, rock, grasshopper. Each person picks a slip of paper and writes a story (any length) about one of the historical events from the view of the animal or object.

Title: **"Make a Story"**

Purpose: To introduce creative writing.

Activity: Group.

Materials: Cards, word and number, piece of posterboard (or cork, peg board and hooks) See illustration.

Procedure: Select one student to pick any number on the board. Take off the top number card and then have the child begin the story using this word. Stop him in the middle of the telling and have another child begin at the same place using the word under the number card he chose. When all the words are uncovered, have each child write a story using the words on the board.

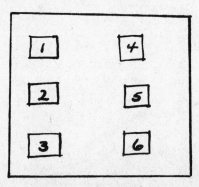

Title:	**"A Diamond of Ideas"**
Purpose:	To give the students ideas for creative writing and to practice creative writing.
Activity:	Group.
Materials:	A blank diamond, divided into four other diamonds, and each with an abstract word written on its perimeter, mimeographed for the class. A similar diamond should be drawn on the board.
Procedure:	Give each child a copy of the blank diamond. Ask them to be thinking of a picture they could draw in each diamond to represent the word written on the diamond. Then, go to the diamond on the board, and ask for some suggestions for pictures to represent the words. Draw one picture in each diamond. Ask the students whose suggestions for pictures you used why they chose those pictures as symbols of the words written on the diamonds.
	Next, ask all students to draw a picture in each diamond on their paper, to represent the word written on the perimeter of the diamond. After they have completed this task, ask them to choose two of the pictures they drew and write a paragraph about them, and tell you why they chose those pictures to represent the words on the diamonds.

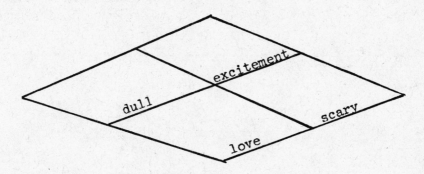

Title:	**"Our Story Book'**
Purpose:	To give the class an exercise for written expression.

Activity: Group.

Materials: The students will need materials for writing stories, illustrating their stories, and binding them into a book.

Procedure: Each student will be asked to write a short story or poem such as a mystery, adventure, or fantasy. The stories should be proofread, corrected, and rewritten. Then divide the class into several groups. Each group will then illustrate the stories, make an index for them, and fashion a decorated cover for its book. The finished books may be displayed for visitors and stories could be read out loud for the class.

Title: **"Humor—Funny Verse"**

Purpose: Creative writing.

Activity: Group.

Procedure: The teacher draws these objects on the board:

Children look at them with eyes of imagination and write a funny verse about what one figure represents.

|

This bald man
Has just one hair
He's just being chased
By a very large bear

This is a clean sheet
That with a thud
Last Munday fell in some
Beautiful mud!

Title:	**"Imagine What Happens"**
Purpose:	Using his imagination, the child will write an ending to a specific situation or story.
Activity:	Group.
Materials:	You may wish to display pictures or posters of the situation or story you are talking about.
Procedure:	The teacher should tell the children that she is going to tell them a story, but this one is a little different because it won't have an ending. She should tell them that she wants them to write an ending for the story themselves.

Title:	**"Our Own Joke Book"**
Purpose:	Developing written expression.
Activity:	Group.
Materials:	Ditto sheet for each child.
Procedure:	Ask each student to think of his favorite joke. After some thought, ask everyone to tell his joke to rest of class. Then give each child a ditto sheet to write his joke on. After he has written a letter-perfect copy, give each child a ditto and have him copy his joke and put his name on it. Run off one copy for each child. Assemble and put into booklet.

Title:	**"Class Poem"**
Purpose:	To introduce children to writing poetry.
Activity:	Group.
Procedure:	In this activity, the class is going to write a poem. One line will be contributed by each class member. Inform the students that they don't have to put their name on their contributions. Ask the class for a few rules to give the poem unity. You might suggest that every line begin with "I wish" and contain a color. Tell the class not to worry about rhyme as it hampers expressive thought at this early stage. Encourage them to take chances and tell them not to worry about being silly. Collect lines from the students and then read them all together as a poem. There will probably be enough humor and fresh imagination to make the experience enjoyable. If the activity is successful, the children will be excited about what the class as a whole has accomplished and may be encouraged to try one on their own.

Title:	**"Film Strip Stories"**
Purpose:	To develop story writing.
Activity:	Group.
Procedure:	Put slide film in your camera and shoot pictures around your school. When sending the film for development, request holes be punched in the sides. Present your filmstrip to the class for a common, vicarious experience, and have each student write a story about his school. You could make other strips when on outings and use them with your class.

Title:	**"The Blob"**
Purpose:	To inspire written expression.
Activity:	Group.
Materials:	A few signs saying "The Blob Is Coming" and a number

of squares of construction paper on which are printed ink blots.

Procedure: Make some ink blots on large sheets of construction paper and print on them, "The Blob Is Coming." Have them hanging in the room about a week before Blob Story Day. Tell the students when Blob Story Day will be in order to promote their curiousity. When the day arrives, have one ink blot for each student on a square of construction paper. Pass one out to each student. When they ask you what they are, tell them that is what you want them to write about.

Title: **"A Visit to the Farm"**

Purpose: To help stimulate children's creative writing through visual aids.

Activity: Group.

Materials: Ditto sheets of animals.

Procedure: The teacher asks the class how many students have ever lived on or visited a farm. She then asks what animals they saw. "Today let's pretend we're going to visit a farm. I am going to hand out a paper with some farm animals on it, and I would like each of you to see if you can put the correct word under each animal. I have a list of the animals at the top of the page. Then let's write a short story about a farm or about visiting a farm including some of the animals in our story.

CHAPTER 7

How to Build Vocabulary as the
Key Foundation for Language
Power with 24 Activities

There is no question about vocabulary development building language power. Acquisition of vocabulary makes students proficient in using their language, and is directly related to reading prowess. Because vocabulary power is the key to all language skill development, teachers work to increase language facility at every grade level. Thus, these 24 creative teaching ideas will be found useful to teachers at all levels.

With such interesting titles as "Letter Card Game," "Football Words," "Go Around the Board," and "Build a Pyramid," your students will be intrigued, motivated, and ready to participate in the activities you provide. Although the chapter organization begins with always interesting gaming activities, which are followed by independent and then by group activities, this arrangement is only for your convenience. While on the basis of the title a game would seem to be of potentially highest interest, group activities are many times the equal of games in sustaining student interest. Selection is best made on the basis of vocabulary needs of your students and what kind of grouping arrangement best facilitates individualized learning.

By making a few changes or adjustments in these prescribed activities, you can oftentimes generate slightly different ones that further enrich your program. For example, "Letter Bingo" has 12 letters in the illustration. By marking different letters on new cards, you can utilize the same idea and expand the vocabulary possibilities.

Since vocabulary development is the responsibility of teachers at every grade level, launch off by using an activity or two a week. See if your students are not stimulated and eager for more.

Title:	**"Pick-a-Slip"**
Purpose:	To increase vocabulary—single words and phrases.
Activity:	Small group game.
Materials:	Print single words or phrases on slips of paper. Write a numerical value from one to three in the upper right-hand corner of each slip.
Procedure:	Two or more people may play. The slips are placed face down on the table. The players take turns selecting a slip and reading it. If the player can read the slip correctly, he keeps the slip. If he does not read it correctly, he replaces the slip face down on the table and the next player takes his turn. The winner is the person who, after all the slips have been picked up, has the highest score by adding the numbers on all the slips.

Title:	**"Letter Bingo"**
Purpose:	To increase vocabulary and word meaning.

BINGO CARD

A	B	C
R	M	Q
K	V	T
P	U	Y

Activity:	Group game.
Materials:	Cards with the alphabet on them, chips or markers, individually cut letters of the alphabet.
Procedure:	Give every child a card and chips. Choose and call a letter from the stack of individually cut letters. The first person to recognize that a word has been spelled and can give a definition or an example of the word meaning wins the game.

Title:	**"Vocabulary"**
Purpose:	To provide practice in vocabulary development.
Activity:	Game.
Procedure:	Assuming children have encountered a number of new words in various contexts, put each new word on a 3 x 8 card, assigning an arbitrary number from 1 to 50 to each card. Cards are to be placed face down on a desk or in the middle of a circle the class may have formed. Children then proceed one at a time or around the circle to draw any card they want, without looking at the face. After choosing a card from the pile, the child turns it over, reads his word, and gives the proper definition. If he gives the proper definition, he receives the number of points beside the word. If not, he merely keeps his previous total. The card is immediately replaced at random in the pile after each player completes his turn. There is a chance that one or several players may choose the same word, but it's really a good drill and to their credit if they remember the definition. After each player has received so many turns, the one with the highest total number of points is the winner and should be given some reward or privilege.

Title:	**"Letter Card Game"**
Purpose:	Develop word usage and widen vocabulary.
Activity:	Game.

Procedure: You need a deck of cards (more if possible) with the alphabet on them. Shuffle the cards so that they are mixed well then deal to 2 or 3 students to a team, having a complete alphabet per team. Then have each team member form as many words as he can from the letters dealt to him. Score a point for every correct word, the team collectively having the highest score wins. The individual with the most points can also be recognized. Or the game can be played shuffling one alphabet between 2 or 3 players and competing individually.

This too could be used for several grades with different things stressed for different weaknesses.

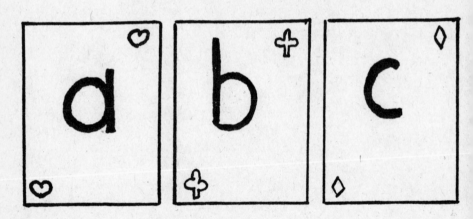

Title: **"Football Words"**

Purpose: To motivate students to learn new vocabulary.

Activity: Group game.

Materials: Word cards.

Procedure: Teacher draws football field on blackboard and divides class into two teams. The teacher has words written on cards. Each team is given cards for each team member. The words on the cards are the same for both teams. The teacher defines a word. The team player who stands up and says the word ahead of the other team member with the same word scores a point for the team.

Example: Teacher: to feel with the hands
                  Word: grasp

Title: **"Definition Bingo"**

Purpose: To give students reinforcement of learning definitions of words.

Activity: Game.

Materials: Bingo cards or ditto sheets, with each having a different word, and some markers.

Procedure: The teacher reads a definition, and the child marks the word on his card which is the answer to the definition. When the child has marked four squares across, down, or vertically, then a child calls out definition, and he is the winner.

dog	cat	school	water
hot	eat	fish	boy
girl	cold	car	math
man	house	father	bird

Definition:

1. an animal that lives in the sea.
2. an animal that flies through the air.

Title: **"Vocabulary Drill"**

Purpose: To increase vocabulary and oral communication.

Activity: Game.

Materials: Game cards.

Procedure: Make a game board as illustrated below. New vocabulary or spelling words may be used around the edge. In the center of the game board, round cards are stacked with instructions on them. The outermost card should be blank. When a card is removed, the student (individual or team member) does what the card indicates as quickly as possible. If synonyms are written on the center card, the participant calls synonyms for the words. Center cards should be labeled synonyms, homonyms, antonyms, use in sentence, and define. Competitors can keep score.

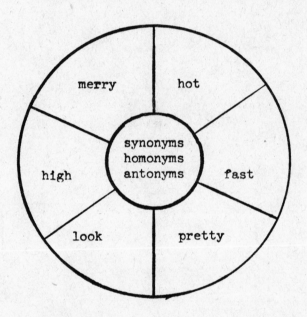

Title:	**"Dolch Relay"**
Purpose:	To give children practice in basic sight words.
Activity:	Game.
Procedure:	Divide the class into two teams. Show a word card taken from the Dolch list. The first child who names the word keeps the card for his team. It is a good idea to have two copies of the word in case both teams get the word at the same time. As soon as a person reads a word, he moves to the back of the line. After all words have been called, the teams count the number of cards that their team has. The team with the most cards is the winner.

Title: **"Go Around the Board"**

Purpose: To provide practice with sight vocabulary and further develop word recognition skills.

Activity: Game for 2-4 people.

Materials: A rectangular piece of heavy paper, 12 inches on each side, with a 2-inch margin. The margin is divided into spaces in which words for practice are written. Some of the spaces may be used for penalties or rewards. A spinner or dice for determining the number of spaces to be moved and a colored marker for each player are necessary.

Procedure: Each player spins the arrow or throws the dice and moves clockwise the number of spaces indicated, starting on "Home Base." He reads the word upon which he lands. If he doesn't know the word, he returns to the original space until his next turn. The child first going all the way around to "Home Base" wins.

MOVE UP 3						MOVE BACK 2	
RETO TO HOME							
							MOVE UP 3
HOME BASE					MOVE BACK 2		MISS 1 TURN

Title:	**"Substitution"**
Purpose:	To give the child practice in vocabulary building.
Activity:	Independent.
Materials:	Story on a chart.
Procedure:	The children as a class read the story together. Then they rewrite the story by changing any words they can by using opposites. Therefore, they change the meaning of the story.
Illustration:	

Chart Story

It was a hot, sticky day in the summer. The sun had been shining bright and warm. John and Mary walked uptown.

Child's Story

It was a cold, calm night in the winter. The rain had been raining dreary and cold. John and Mary stayed inside.

Title:	**"Who Lives Here?"**
Purpose:	To give children practice in distinguishing antonyms, synonyms, homonyms.

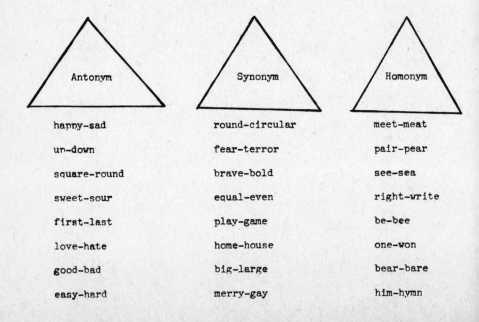

Antonym	Synonym	Homonym
happy-sad	round-circular	meet-meat
up-down	fear-terror	pair-pear
square-round	brave-bold	see-sea
sweet-sour	equal-even	right-write
first-last	play-game	be-bee
love-hate	home-house	one-won
good-bad	big-large	bear-bare
easy-hard	merry-gay	him-hymn

Activity:	Independent.
Materials:	Ditto sheets, pencil.
Procedure:	Discuss how some words are like people. People have homes and some words have homes. Have children draw outlines of three homes on paper. (Or you prepare ditto.) Label them Antonym, Synonym, and Homonym Homes. Ask the children to fill in the homes with as many antonyms, synonyms, and homonyms as they can think of.

Title:	**"Build a Pyramid"**
Purpose:	To encourage the writing of new words for vocabulary development.
Activity:	Individual.
Procedure:	Write three vowels on the chalkboard and have students copy them on their papers. Explain that the letter is the top of the pyramid and they must build down by adding one letter to any part of the word. By adding just one letter to each line they can build a pyramid.

```
        E                          A
       B E                        A M
      B E T                      R A M
     B E S T                    R E A M
    B E A S T                  R E A L M

                      O
                     O R
                    O R B
                   O R B S
                  O R B I T
```

Title:	**"More About Words"**
Purpose:	Vocabulary Enrichment
Activity:	Individual or small group.

Materials: Ditto of following crossword puzzle.

Procedure: Children solve the puzzle by choosing from a given list of
                 words.

Illustration: amaze   lazy
                    blaze   magazine
                    breeze   prize
                    citizen   sneeze
                    freeze   zebra
                    froze   zigzag
                    graze   zoo
                    grief

Across: Down:

2. Sorrow   1. Member of a town, city,
4. Something to read   state
6. A flame   2. To feed on grass
7. A soft wind   3. To become frozen
9. The cold _____ my nose   5. To surprise
                                            8. A collection of animals

Across:	2. grief	4. magazine	6. blaze
	7. breeze	9. froze	
Down:	1. citizen	2. graze	3. freeze
	5. amaze	8. zoo	

Title:	**"Matching Synonyms"**
Purpose:	To increase vocabulary power.
Activity:	Independent.
Materials:	Two sets of cards on which words are printed. One set of words is matched by a set of matching synonyms.
Procedure:	Each card in set I is placed down in a vertical column, and then the synonyms from set II are laid beside the words that have the same meaning.
Illustration:	sad _____ unhappy brave _____ unafraid

Title:	**"Opposites"**
Purpose:	As a result of the activity, the children will: show ability in distinguishing opposites demonstrate extent of their vocabulary.
Activity:	Individual or group.

Materials: Prepare twenty 3 x 5 cards with ten pairs of word opposites. One of each set of words should be displayed on a flannel board or other device, the remaining words displayed across the bottom of board.

Procedure: The class will be instructed to match the proper opposite words either on a separate sheet of paper or aloud in front of the class. From time to time the words can be changed around and new words substituted.

FLANNELBOARD WITH CARDS READY FOR USE

hot				
big				
up				
on				
short				
fat				
night				
dry				
white				
cool				
day	off	cold	warm	black
little	down	thin	wet	tall

Title.   **"Rest Box"**

Purpose: The purpose of this activity is to make the students aware of words in our language that can substitute (with more accurate meaning) for overused words.

Activity: Group.

Procedure: On one bulletin board have an illustration of a box labeled, "Rest Box." Alert the students to watch for frequent usage of worn-out words and phrases such as, "nice," "good," "can," "made," and "to go." When the word is heard used in the classroom, it is written on a tag and placed in the rest box. This is followed by a discussion in the class to find a substitute word with a more accurate and descriptive meaning. Keep the list of the substitute outside the box, using an arrangement like the one below.

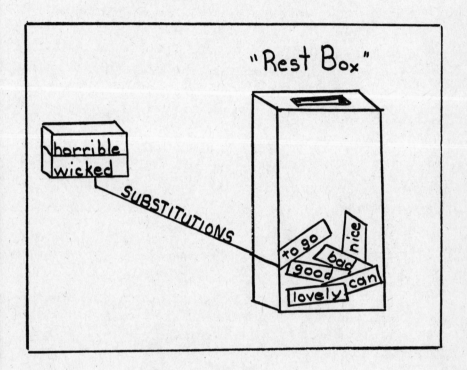

Title:	**"Vocabulary Builders"**
Purpose:	To build vocabularies.
Activity:	Group.
Materials:	Newspapers, magazines, radio, television, other communication media.
Procedure:	1. The students keep a "diary" of unknown or unfamiliar words which they hear on television, radio, etc. or which they find in the newspaper, magazines, or books.

2. The students compile their lists to find the most common or frequent words.

3. Working on ten words at a time, the students study their spelling, definition, and pronunciation.

4. Special recognition should be given when these words appear in speech or writing as an incentive for the students to place these words in their vocabulary.

This is an excellent exercise for culturally disadvantaged or diverse students in an effort to acquaint them with the commonly accepted or used language. This is valuable in correcting pronunciation problems due to colloquialisms or slang.

Title:	**"Classroom Password"**
Purpose:	To develop vocabularies.
Activity:	Game.
Materials:	3 x 5 cards, file boxes for each student. Cards are numbered in the upper corners on both sides.
Procedure:	Children record words introduced by the teacher from various sources on 3 x 5 cards. Each child owns a file box in which the cards are kept. The cards are numbered in the upper corners on both sides. In the center of the card is printed the new word. Directly beneath the word, in parentheses, is printed the phonetic spelling in syllables with the proper diacritical marks. At the bottom of this side of the card, the child uses the word in a sentence he has made up. On the reverse side of the card, he writes the definition of the word.

When pupils begin to build up a file of words, the game PASSWORD (based on the TV game of the same name) can be employed. The teacher acts as moderator. Four pupils are chosen, two opposing another couple. Two sets of cards are used. The teacher gives a same-numbered card to a pupil on each team. The pupil of the team chosen to begin gives a one-word synonym clue to his partner who attempts to name the word within a reasonable amount of time and only one attempt.

If correct, 10 points are awarded that team and another word is selected with the opposite team beginning. If incorrect, the other team tries for nine points. If neither answers correctly, each side alternates in attempts for one point less each time until there are no points left.

A new word is then selected and the procedure begins again. When a team answers correctly, another word is selected by the teacher and given to the pupils on each team who attempted the correct word previously. When a team amasses 25 points, the game if over and a new team or teams are selected.

Round-robin tournaments can be established. After all teams have played, an elimination can be established with winning teams and losing teams, if so desired. Other pupils may participate by keeping a running score for each team on the chalkboard; acting as judges to determine whether clues are acceptable; or as moderators in place of the teacher.

Title:	**"Mythology Dictionary"**
Purpose:	To research the history of words that come from myths and speculate on the modern day expression.
Activity:	Group.
Materials:	Dictionaries, Books of Myths, *Words from the Myths* by Isaac Asimov.
Procedure:	Introduce the children to several books of myths. Discuss some of them and ask students about a particular word—What word do we know that resembles it? What does it mean today? Then, have them check the word in the dictionary.

Divide the class into groups and let each group select several myths to choose words from and research them. (*Words from Myths* will help them.) As the words are researched, let them compile a notebook listing the words and their meanings with the modern day word or expression.

Length of time for this project is flexible. Finally, have

each group submit their list to the class. Let the children who wish serve on a committee to alphabetize and compile a classroom dictionary that all the students can enjoy.

Examples: 1. Brontes: Mythical Greek monster whose name meant thunder (brontosaurus).

2. Furies: The terrible goddesses of vengeance who punished people for every kind of crime (fury, furious).

3. Midas: A king who had the power to change all he touched to gold. This blessing became a curse (the Midas Touch).

Title: **"Vocabulary"**

Purpose: To help the students expand and add variety to their spelling and writing vocabulary.

Activity: Group.

Materials: All that is needed are a blackboard, a poster, and writing materials for the class.

Procedure: The instructor begins by writing a word on the blackboard and asking the class to name as many words as they can to describe it or how they feel about it. These words

POSTER

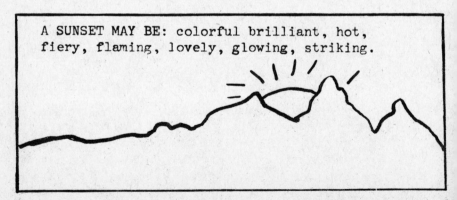

could then compose one week's spelling lesson. The class should next write a story which uses these words and each story can be hung around a poster which illustrates the lesson.

Illustration: Word given: SUNSET
List: colorful, brilliant, hot, lovely,
       glowing, fiery, flaming, striking, etc.

Title: **"Homonym Tree"**

Purpose: To help the children build their vocabulary through oral communication.

Activity: Group.

Materials: A poster containing a picture of a homonym tree with

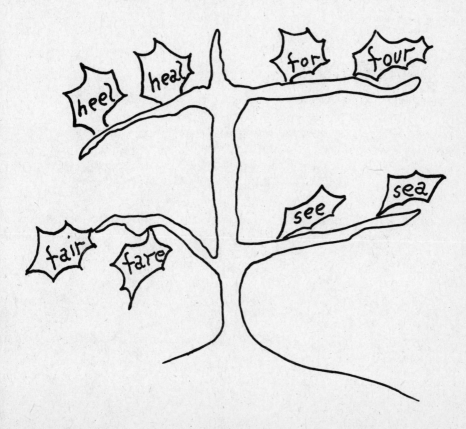

leaves containing the names of the homonyms. See illustration.

Procedure:	Begin by telling the children that they are going to get to do something special in which they will have an opportunity to do the talking. Then give the directions for the activity: Show the children the homonym tree and tell them that they will be using these words to do the activity. Tell the children they will be divided into groups of two and each group will have a chance to make up a conversation in which they use two of the words from the homonym tree during the conversation. Divide the children into groups and let them work on a conversation. The teacher will then pick on several groups to say their conversation.

Title:	**"Vocabulary Week"**
Purpose:	To develop vocabulary.
Activity:	Group.
Procedure:	The teacher sets aside one week during each report card period as "new vocabulary week." During this week each student is asked to bring at least three words that he finds new and interesting to him from magazines, newspapers, television, or from verbal contact with family, neighbors, or relatives. These new words will be deposited in a special new vocabulary box from which the teacher will draw each word and write it on the blackboard and then allow students to vote on the 30 most interesting words the class will learn.

Title:	**"Bulletin Board"**
Purpose:	To get across the point that many words have more than one meaning.
Activity:	Group.

Procedure: The attached sketch is for a bulletin board. The word *hard* is an example of a word that has more than one meaning.

MANY WORDS HAVE SEVERAL MEANINGS

"The accident was a bit of hard luck"

WHAT DOES THE WORD HARD MEAN?

HARD WORK

HARD-HEARTED

HARD CASH

HARD AS NAILS

HARD AND FAST

Title:	**"What's the Category?"**
Purpose:	Development of vocabulary concepts.
Activity:	Group.
Procedure:	Make a list of sets of words. Each set contains four words all of which can be grouped into a single category. Let the class read the sets of words. Have children see if they can find the correct word for which all the words will apply. These words or categories must be precise. Do not accept a phrase for a single word.

Examples:

1. factory barn house silo   (buildings)
2. car bus boat plane   (vehicles)
3. ring bracelet necklace pin   (jewelry)
4. pint yard bushel inch   (units of measure)
5. penny nickle dime quarter   (coins)
6. wheat corn oats barley   (grain)
7. boot shoe sock slipper   (footwear)
8. baseball golf tennis hockey   (sports)

9. Washington Monroe Johnson Ford   (presidents)
10. chocolate licorice jellybean lollypop   (candy)
11. George Sally Albert Stella   (names)
12. love happiness hate fright   (feelings)
13. hammer rake saw hoe   (tools)
14. wall fence dam dike   (barriers)
15. circle square oval triangle   (shapes)
16. orange purple green red   (colors)
17. Mars Jupiter Neptune Saturn   (planets)
18. ocean river lake sea   (bodies of water)

CHAPTER 8

Applying Creative Dramatics to
the Classroom Through 28 Activities

Creative teachers have long been using dramatics in their classrooms as imaginative learning activities. From impromptu skits through creative dramatics and theatrical display, children have been learning communication skills in exciting, active environments. It is in this kind of activity that children use all of their language skills, for they speak with expression, listen, read their parts, and write their scripts. Then too, teachers frequently use a dramatic activity as a vehicle to emphasize highlights of history, scientific inventions, and to convey important concepts to their young scholars. Needless to say, creative dramatics has many functional uses, particularly in the development of children's language skills, and should never be considered a frill, but a valuable learning strategy.

In this chapter you will find numerous dramatic activities to help you set the stage for communication skill development. Your students will enthusiastically immerse themselves in these valuable learning activities because children by nature are expressive and take delight in projecting their personalities. From "Silent Skits," through "Fun at the Circus," and many others, your students will enjoy using and developing their language skills. And particularly those shy, retiring children will have many pleasant opportunities to come out from behind their shutters and learn that satisfaction is derived from open expression.

There are other ancillary benefits to utilizing dramatics in your program. By the nature of dramatics, people interact socially, and these experiences of mingling and cooperating facilitate the acquisition of social skills, getting along with one another, and respecting each person's personal worth.

Survey the activities in this chapter, and choose one or two for use next week. You might use one in your social studies unit and another in your language arts program. Once your children are involved, their contagious, enthusiastic participation will reveal that dramatic activity is a language-learning vehicle unmatched by any other teaching strategy.

Title:	**"Raindrops Keep Falling On My Head" (Puppet Show)**
Purpose:	To illustrate a simple way of making puppets and using puppetry. Puppetry is a fascinating art which all children enjoy. It can help children gain a self concept, can aid the children in making reports, and can aid the teacher in many ways.
	Puppets, however fun and useful, can be difficult to make. This is an illustration of how simple puppets can be.
Activity:	Group.
Materials:	*Puppets:*

Styrofoam balls (different sizes)
yarn (for hair)
felt
construction paper
scrap material (for costume)
paints
parts of old teddy bears

Stage
cardboard box
contact paper
cloth for curtain

Special Effects
Tape Recorder
Aluminum foil glove (rain)

Procedure:

1. Explanation of how the puppets are constructed.

2. Explain the purpose of the tape recorder.

3. Introduce characters

4. Puppet show . . . .

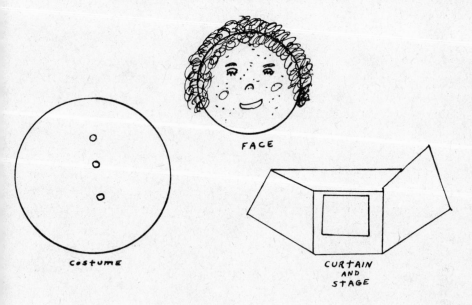

FACE

COSTUME

CURTAIN
AND
STAGE

Title:	**"Assume a Role"**
Purpose:	Dramatic expression.
Procedure:	Have the children dramatize the action suggested by a paragraph. Tell the children that you're going to read them a paragraph from their unit—such as, one about an animal in a circus unit. Tell them to listen carefully, and when you've finished you will choose someone to pretend to be the animal and act out what you read to them, in the exact order that you read it. Will you be the one to get it just right? Listen!! Begin with one or two sentences and increase the number as the listening efficiency increases.
Illustration:	A lion paced slowly back and forth in its cage. Suddenly he stopped stock-still and listened. Then he sniffed the air. Then he gave a low growl and lay down on the floor of his cage.

Title:	**"Puppet Skit"**
Purpose:	Development of skills in creative thinking, written expression, and dramatic expression.
Activity:	Group.
Materials:	Several puppets.
Procedure:	Give the children puppets and divide them into small groups. Each group should develop a short skit about these characters. Allow as much time as needed to prepare these skits. Each group will be given a chance to present its skit the following day.

Title:	**"Acting Out"**
Purpose:	To give children an experience of acting out short stories, songs, or poems as an opportunity for creative development.
Activity:	Group.
Materials:	Ditto of the story, song, or poem.
Procedure:	Give the children a story on a ditto sheet or read them a story. Then have the children take turns expressing dramatically what they have read or heard.
Illustration:	LITTLE BOY

This little boy is going to bed
    Down on the pillow he lays his head
Wraps himself up in the covers tight
    And this is the way he sleeps all night,

Morning comes, he opens his eyes
    And back with a toss the covers fly
Up he jumps, is dressed, and away
    Ready to frolic and play all day.

Title:	**"Mixed Up Pictures"**
Purpose:	To develop communication skills.

Activity: Group.

Materials: Several pictures that show different parts of the story.

Procedure: Divide class into groups. Show each group two pictures (the first picture to each group plus one different picture to each group). Let each group decide how they will act out the story their group sees in the two pictures they have. Let groups perform and then discuss differences and what caused them. Then view all pictures and discuss possible stories.

Title: **"Animal Characters"**

Purpose: Development of skills in dramatic expression.

Activity: Group.

Procedure: Read a story about different animals and then have a child come forward. Whisper to the child the animal you want him to imitate physically. The other children will try and guess the name of the animal.

Title.   **"Sign Language"**

Purpose: Development of non-verbal expression skills.

Activity: Group.

Procedure: Ask the children if they know anything about sign language. Have them use their hands to say stop, go, wave, and to show that they are sleepy. Then let different children act out pantomines and have the rest of the class guess what it is they are doing. (Example: brushing teeth, mowing the lawn, rocking a baby, and catching a fish.)

Title: **"Expression"**

Purpose: The students will listen and use dramatics to illustrate what they hear.

Activity: Group.

Materials: A short action story.

Procedure: Tell the class to listen very carefully as you read a short action story. Select a student for each character in the story and have them come up in front of the class. There can be characters for things like wind or rain. They are to act out the story as it is read again. If the teacher wishes to have the students act on the first reading of the story, then she may do so.

Title: **"Tell a Tale"**

Purpose: To aid in developing creative expression.

Activity: Group.

Materials: Six folders with a variety of pictures in them. Tape recorder.

Procedure: Give out the folders containing pictures to the students, but tell the students in advance not to open the folders until called upon. The teacher starts telling a story. She points to a student with a folder. He looks at his picture and continues telling the story. His part of the story should be related to his picture. The rest of the students do the same as it comes their turn. The last child ends the story. Tape the activity and play it back for the students.

Title: **"Shoes"**

Purpose: Development of creative expression.

Activity: Group.

Materials: About ten pairs of old shoes, both men's and women's.

Procedure: Have children dramatize a story they have read, created on their own or an idea that you have given them. When they become a character, they put on the shoes that the character would probably wear. Have groups perform for each other. Also, this could be done using different hats.

Title:	**"Creative Dramatics Through Puppetry"**
Purpose:	To help students to express their ideas, feelings, and emotions through verbal and dramatic play.
Activity:	Group.
Procedure:	Ask for students to volunteer to role-play with puppets. They should discuss briefly their coordination of characters, plot, and scenery. After a few moments to acquaint themselves with the puppets, their manipulation, and their position in the set, they give their characterization of the story THE THREE BILLY GOATS GRUFF in their own words. Give all other students opportunity to use the puppets in performance.

Culmination: Discuss other ways to use the puppets and then decide what other stories could be used to suit puppetry. Consider rhymes and poems.

Put these puppets in a shoebox and label. Put on a shelf with other directing activities that students can play with at various times. The puppets are sturdy and should last a long time. Eventually get several boxes with characters in them. Make many different types of puppets.

Title:	**"Sell It"**
Purpose:	To stimulate creative thinking and develop creative expression.
Activity:	Group.
Materials:	A made-up object. For example, a jar with a flower on top or a book with a hole through the center of it.
Procedure:	The teacher places some interesting object, which she has constructed, in front of the class. She tells the class that the purpose of this activity is to make a commercial to sell a product. The product is the teacher's constructed object. The creative ideas are to be written on the blackboard. The commercial can be written as a song or a

play. The students can act out the commercial for another class or for an assembly program.

Title:	**"Puppets"**
Purpose:	To develop self expression.
Activity:	Group.
Materials:	Paper bags or cloth, needles, and thread to make the puppets, a large carton for the stage.
Procedure:	Selections for dramatizing can come from several sources. The story can originate with the class, a book which you have just read or would like the class to read, or an excerpt from history, a safety lesson, a lesson in manners, a health program, or any topic of interest. Allow the students to choose what they would like to work on: writing the story, making the puppets, staging sound effects, making the props, or whatever.
Example:	The class might work up a presentation on George Washington as part of their history lesson and present it in February. This would give the student an opportunity to study the dress of the time as well as an in-depth study of the contribution of the "Father of Our Country."

Title:	**"Traits"**
Purpose:	Free expression in the development of personality traits; a relaxed atmosphere among peers in the classroom.
Activity:	Group.
Materials:	A typed description of each character's traits along with a cutout of each animal character that is portraying a human personality trait but is conveyed through an animal "form."
Procedure:	This is an acting out of different character types in the form of a "game." Each child picks a character (with description and dialogue attached). Each child will act out his or her part *independently* of, but within, the total group. Role taking!

Start the lesson by asking the students if they have ever wanted to be someone or something else. Have a relaxing session and ask them what they feel like at that moment. Then have ten "volunteers" come forward and each child pick an animal (human trait) character at random and each child act out his specific part.

Illustration: Cutouts could include:

1. A "stately" deer
2. A chipmunk with an allergy
3. A shy mouse
4. A blind mole that hums
5. A forgetful squirrel
6. An opossum
7. A worldly male rabbit
8. A prissy female rabbit
9. A fine "ole Southern gentleman" rabbit
10. A "little boy" rabbit

Title: **"Listen To Me"**

Purpose: Develop self expression through play acting.

Activity: Small group.

Materials: Large refrigerator box, paint.

Procedure: Build a television set out of a large cardboard box and cut a hole so it looks like a TV. Next, make a small door in the back so the children can come and go through the back. This allows the child to play-act anyone or anything he wishes in front of the whole class or just a small audience. He may tell them what he did the previous day, or about a new pet, etc.

Title: **"Finger Plays"**

Purpose: To help development of expression.

Activity: Group.

Materials: Poems that the class can say and "participate" in.

Procedure: As the class says the poem, have them also put actions with it.

Illustration: The following poem is good to use for this type of activity:

> Two tall telephone poles
> > (point fingers erect)
> Between them a wire is strung
> > (two middle fingers touching)
> Two birds hopped on
> > (press thumb against middle finger)
> And swung, swung, swung,
> > (sway arms back and forth)

Title: **"Paperbag Production"**

Purpose: To provide oral communication practice using dramatic creativity. This would give the child an opportunity better to learn how to work with a group.

Activity: Small groups of five or six with the entire class participating in a group.

Materials: Five or six large paper bags containing five or six items.

Procedure: The groups will take five minutes to create some story where they would use each of the articles contained in the paper bag. More time may be given depending on the groups' progression. Individually, the groups will put on their production for the rest of the class practicing good listening habits.

Title: **"Pantomime"**

Purpose: To give students pantomime experience.

Activity: Group.

Procedure: Give each student a card with the name of a person or historical event on it. Give them a few minutes to mentally plan their pantomimes. As each one presents his pantomime, the rest of the class tries to guess who or what he represents.

For instance, if the class is studying the Civil War, you could use Robert E. Lee, U.S. Grant, a Southern belle, a plantation owner, some of the battles, etc.

Title: **"Drama On Film"**

Purpose: The purpose of this activity is to give the class the opportunity to express themselves dramatically, and to evaluate themselves when the movie is played back.

Activity: Group.

Materials: Film projector, movie camera (8mm home movie set is recommended), a screen, and a tape recorder.

Procedure: The class should have a play or write one. They should rehearse it prior to filming. After it has been taped and filmed, the class should evaluate themselves objectively.

Example: One suggested subject that could be used is a historical figure's life or a period of his life that is interesting.

Title: **"Writing a Dramatization for Puppets"**

Purpose: To practice oral expression, writing a dramatic presentation, and working with a group.

Activity: Group.

Materials: A list of short stories familiar to the class and suitable for translation to a dramatic presentation, construction paper or small paper bags, crayons, and an example of a short story translated into a dramatic presentation.

Procedure: Ask the class the difference between a play and a short story. Then, with a short story familiar to the class, ask them how you should go about making the short story into a play. Suggest to the class the role of narrator to connect unsequential scenes in the play. Then, with the class, rewrite the short story. Next, divide the class into heterogeneous groups. Tell each group they are to select a short story to rewrite into a play for presentation with puppets. Offer them a list of short stories to choose from.

but tell them they may choose one not on the list. After a short time, ask each group which story they have chosen, so they won't spend much time on selection of a story. Tell them they will be allowed three periods to work on the play; one, to write it; two, to select and practice roles, and for those students, who have small roles or no roles, to make puppets; and, three, to present the plays.

Illustration: The puppets may be faces drawn on small paper bags or faces drawn on two pieces of construction paper, cut in the shape of a puppet, stapled or pasted together at the edges, and with a pleat down each side.

The Golden Touch

(Midas is counting his gold.)

King Midas: "There is no greater enjoyment in the world than counting one's gold. If only I had more, my enjoyment would be ten-times increased."

(His daughter, the princess, enters with flowers.)

Princess: "Father, I brought you some flowers. Aren't they beautiful?"

King Midas: "Yes, they are pretty, but not as beautiful as my wealth of golden coins."

     etc.

Title:	**"Christmas in Other Lands"**
Purpose:	To develop students' dramatic abilities. Dramatize Christmas in other lands.
Activity:	Group.
Procedure:	Discuss with class Christmas in other lands. Divide class into five groups, and give each a country to dramatize how they celebrate Christmas. Allow time for props to be made. Each group should keep its country a secret until the day they perform before the class. The rest of the

class will try to guess which country the group is representing.

There are many books with stories of Christmas in other lands. Example: Swiss children place one shoe outside the door two Saturdays before Christmas. If they have been good they will find candy and nuts in their shoes. Christmas Eve they go to bed early and wake the next morning to find a loaded Christmas tree.

Title: **"Body Communication"**

Purpose: To encourage and develop non-verbal expression as a prelude to dramatic activities.

Procedure: Let students take turns in portraying (through actions only) some type of activity while the class tries to guess what they are doing.

Illustration: Eating a banana
Eating spaghetti
Hanging clothes on a line
Sweeping the floor
Painting a picture
Cutting flowers
Typing a letter
Wrapping a package
Jumping a rope
Petting a dog

Title: **"Radio Dramatization"**

Purpose: To stimulate use of the imagination, bring out shy children and those who normally don't volunteer for plays and group activities, as well as giving practice in reading with expression and role acting.

Activity: Group.

Materials: Tape recorder, tape, materials required for sound effects (or reasonable facsimiles), copies of the play for each child. Select a play from a reader or another source.

Procedure:	Use as many children as possible. Be sure participants read the play ahead of time and understand their parts. Use some students who are not in the play as sound effects people or for crowd scenes. Have an announcer and even commercials. Tape the play—it is easy to erase and re-do one person's part and get immedate results. Different groups could do the same play or other ones.
Title:	**"Help Me Find My Way"**
Purpose:	Development of oral expression, organization of thought patterns and dramatic play.
Activity:	Group.
Procedure:	Teacher has typed up different cards for the group of four. Each group has its leader draw a card. On the card is printed the name of one place where a child might lose his way, such as a department store. Everyone also may be given a list of questions to direct his thinking with respect to his plea when lost in that particular place, saying in begging tone, "Help me find my way!"

These are their questions for direction:

1. Did I have any instructions before this time with regard to what I should do if lost? If so, what were they?
2. What could I do to picture in my mind where I last saw the person that I came with and from whom I am lost?
3. In this certain place, what written instructions would direct me? What landmarks are a help?

Each member in the group works individually at first, jotting down his thoughts in answer to the questions. After a given length of time, sharing of ideas takes place. As a group they decide on the method of presentation of their ideas to the entire class. As a result of this presentation, the class should better be able to deal with a real life possibility of "getting lost" as well as the language arts values derived therefrom.

Illustration:	Typed cards with these places suggested:

on a street corner
in a new school

in a mall
in a movie theater
in the grocery store
in a large church
in a new neighborhood
on the highway
in a city park

For example:

department store

Title:	**"Commercials"**
Purpose:	To give the children a chance to express themselves creatively.
Activity:	Group.
Materials:	Materials which each group decides it will need for their act.
Procedure:	The class is divided into smaller groups. Each group thinks of a TV commercial they would like to act out. They rehearse, and then present the commercial to the rest of the class. Afterward, the groups make up their own commercials and present them to the class. The class can judge which is better, the homemade one or the commercial TV one.
Illustration:	A soap commercial on TV. Study math it builds knowledge.

Title:	**"Pantomime Your Favorite Folk Song"**
Purpose:	To promote creative expression and to develop appreciation for the meaning of folk songs.
Activity:	Group.
Materials:	A list of American folk songs would get the children thinking about which ones are their favorite. Give them time to gather some props and think about the pantomime act.

Procedure: Have the students divide into groups of four and decide among their groups which song each would like to pantomime. They should be encouraged to work cooperatively when more than one person is needed to do the pantomiming.

Illustration: One group may imitate chain gang actions for "I've Been Working on the Railroad."

Title: **"Speaking and Listening via Puppets"**

Purpose.   To develop expressional skills.

Activity: Group.

Materials: Tape recorder, construction paper, glue, scissors, buttons, scraps of material, thread, yarn, needles, empty cereal boxes, paper bags, and crayons.

Procedure: First the teacher introduces activity with puppets and story. The children then decide upon the type of story or activity they will use. The needed materials are then gathered and the work on the puppets begins. The children then present their story or activity with the puppets.

Title: **"Fun at the Circus"**

Purpose: To develop creative expression.

Activity: Group.

Materials: Hats to distinguish different roles.

Procedure: Have various students role-play the different people in a circus. Such people as the ticket man, the lion tamer, etc. can be dramatized. Hats or objects that the children make themselves can be used. This is an activity in which the entire class can take part.

CHAPTER 9

40 Activities That Teach Word Recognition Skills for Decoding Written Language

Reading is a language skill composed of many sub-skills. These sub-skills are conveniently classified as word recognition and comprehension skills. Students learn word recognition skills to help them identify words and understand the meanings of the words. In this chapter, you will find learning activities which enable children to develop their word recognition skills.

For your convenience and to aid you in selecting specific activities to meet precise skill needs of your students, five sub-headings are used in this chapter. These sections are: sight word recognition, structural analysis, phonics, dictionary skills, and vocabulary relationships. Thus, if you need to teach affixes, roots, and inflectional endings, you can easily locate the activities related to these skills.

Each of these five sections contains gaming ideas, group and independent activities to assist you further in individualizing your instructional program. For example, if you should have several children who need to learn blends, you could select "Consonant Blend Bingo" as a gaming activity to meet the skill needs of those students. They could even play this game without you if you would appoint a capable student to moderate the game. This would free you for working with other students. In the event an individual needs to learn initial sounds, you could select an independent activity such as "Phonic Wheel" for individual work. By knowing the specific skill needs of your students, you can truly meet their instructional needs by individualizing your program.

These teaching ideas are functional with any reading program you are using because they give you learning strategies that complement the instructional material contained in all programs. Every reading program focuses on word recognition skill development and specifically on these five skill areas. Thus, you will not only be able to supplement your program with other learning activities, but you will have the flexibility of meeting individual and group needs to a far greater degree than any program can provide. In addition, should you be using criterion-reference instruments to identify precise skill needs of each student, your word recognition activities can be correlated directly to the criteria.

Begin using these activities gradually by selecting an activity to meet a precise word recognition skill need of one or more of your students. Observe their enthusiasm for learning and evaluate the learning that results. Then you will know the thrill that individualized instruction brings to you and your students.

SIGHT WORD RECOGNITION

Title: **"Dress the Clown"**

Purpose: To develop sight vocabulary.

Activity: Game.

Procedure: This activity aids in word recognition. The teacher should draw a clown on a large sheet of paper. The costume is only outlined. If the child can pronounce the word, he is allowed to place his word on the clown's costume. The child who knows the most words wins the game.

Title: **"Concentration Game"**

Purpose: To introduce new words, spelling words, endings, plurals, etc.

Activity: Game for groups (up to 10) or can be used independently. The number of pairs of cards can be adjusted to suit the size of the group.

Materials: Pairs of cards with desired words printed upon them. A board with nails from which cards can be hung is optional. This method is very good when used with a larger group or introducing new words or when teacher wishes to keep rein over the game.

Procedure: Cards are placed face down at random on a table or hung from board. Students take two cards and turn them over looking for a match. The word must be spoken aloud and spelled, if desired. The cards are turned over again if they don't match, and the next child tries. The cards can be numbered, if desired, to help children choose. This would be necessary if children are not to leave their seats.

Title: **"Word Baseball'**

Purpose: To increase sight vocabulary.

Activity: Game.

Procedure: Divide the class into two teams. The teacher is usually the pitcher. Have the words on flash cards prepared ahead of time. Set up the bases around the room. Pick a scorekeeper and have him keep the score on the blackboard, so it will be visible to all.

As each child comes up to bat, the pitcher flashes a card for the batter to identify the word. If correct, the batter moves to first base. All hits are singles. If wrong, that is an out for that team. Three outs per team per inning.

Variations: This game could be adapted to spelling.

Title:	**"Postman, Postman"**
Purpose:	To help students recall sight words.
Activity:	Game.
Procedure:	Teacher plays part as postman: students as mail callers. Students say,, "Postman, postman do I have any mail today?" The postman says, "I don't know, what's your name?" The postman then shows the pupil a word card. If the pupil responds correctly, the postman replies, "Yes, you have a letter today," and he gives the word card to pupil.

If pupil responds incorrectly, the postmaster answers, "I'm sorry you do not have any mail today." That player's turn is finished and the next student calls for his mail.

As pupils get familiar with game, the child with the most letters at the end of game can assume position of postman.

Title:	**"Little Words"**
Purpose:	To help children learn basic sight words.
Activity:	Small group.
Procedure:	This is a game to help beginning readers learn difficult sight words. Using 3" X 5" cards, the teacher writes each word on one card for each child. The teacher calls out a word, and the children hold up what they think is the correct card. Periodic use of these cards will help reinforce these words in the children's sight vocabularies.

Many children have little trouble remembering nouns and verbs, but they seem to have much difficulty remembering "little words."

Title:	**"Call My Letter"**
Purpose:	To help children learn sight words.
Activity:	Group.
Materials:	Clear plastic. Solid color self-stick plastic. Basic sight words (we, he, she, I, pet, and, me, let, wet, is)
Procedure:	Make aprons out of clear plastic. Use self-stick plastic to cut out letters that make basic sight words. Stick one letter on each apron.
	Put an apron on each child. Call for "Mr. M." The child who is "M" will come forward. Call for "Mr. E." The child who is "E" will come forward. Place the children side by side. The other children will pronounce the word made by the "M" and "E" children. Proceed with the other basic sight words.

Title:	**"Word Match"**
Purpose:	To provide practice in recognition of contractions.
Activity:	Game.
Materials:	Construction paper.
Procedure.	Give cards on which a contraction is written on construction paper to half of the students. Give the other students cards on which are written two words from which one of the contractions is formed. Call on one child to be "It." "It" stands in the middle of a circle of chairs occupied by students. As the teacher says either a contraction or a combination of two words, the child who holds the card with the contraction, and the child who holds the card with the two words change seats. "It" tries to get a seat. The child who does not get a seat then becomes "It."

Title:	**"Spiral Trail"**
Purpose:	To give students practice in identifying sight word vocabulary.

Activity: Game.

Materials: A game board with squares marked off in spiral fashion
                   leading from "start" to "win." Each square has a vo-
                   cabulary word written on it. Use a die or a bag of num-
                   bers. Use any small token for markers.

Procedure: Each player in turn throws die (or draws number from
                   bag) to determine the number of spaces he may move.
                   (Bag of numbers can be used to limit moves to fewer
                   spaces.) Player must identify word he lands on. If he fails
                   to do so he must go back to "start." First player to reach
                   "win" wins. Cardboard game card may be replaced with
                   one having new words as needed.

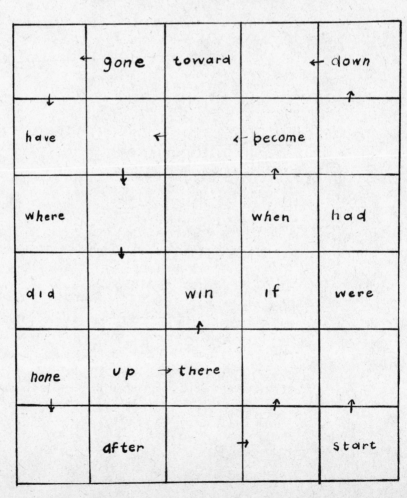

Title: **"Word Puzzle"**

Purpose: To help the students with sight words.

Activity: Independent—each student has a word puzzle. The students try to find all of the words. The student who finds the most words wins.

Procedure: 1. Find the words in the puzzle.

2. All of the words have to do with school.

3. Place a circle around the words.

4. Some of the words read top to bottom.

5. Some of the words read bottom to top.

6. Some of the words read left to right.

7. Some of the words read right to left.

8. The student who finds the most words wins.

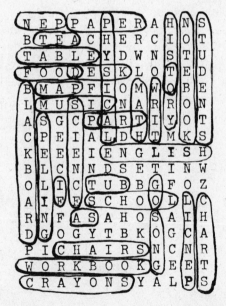

4. <u>Top to bottom</u>   5. <u>Bottom to top</u>

S   L

C   O

H   O

O   H

O   C

L   S

6. <u>Left to right</u>   7. <u>Right to left</u>

SCHOOL   LOOHCS

Variation: Space words, spelling words, sight words, animals, antonyms, flowers.

STRUCTURAL ANALYSIS

Title:	**"Affixes Tag"**
Purpose:	To give practice in using prefixes and suffixes to build new words.
Activity:	Independent.
Materials:	Paper, dictionaries (one per child).
Procedure:	Print approximately 20 words, such as these—shout, give, write, run, etc., at the top of sheets of paper. Have pupils select a word from the stack and change it in as many ways as they can by adding prefixes and suffixes. Tell the children that they may use the dictionaries. After the prescribed period, ask students to share with the class the words they have made.

```
          help
          ____

     help ful
     help ing
     help less
     help er
```

Title:	**"Suffix and Prefix Game"**
Purpose:	To provide an introduction, review and/or recognition of suffixes and prefixes.
Activity:	Independent, in pairs, or small groups.

Materials: Manila envelopes, construction paper (or anything to put the prefixes and suffixes on).

Procedure: Students will look at the root words and select the proper suffix and prefix to put in the blank by the word.

_____ happy	form _____
_____ certain	work _____
_____ equal	clean _____
_____ clean	read _____
Pocket	Pocket

un	er
un	er
un	er
un	er

dis _____	_____ ly
un _____	_____ ness
re _____	_____ est
Pockets	Pockets

tell	fill
kind	cover
dark	cover

Title: **"Tachistoscope"**

Purpose: To teach recognition of affixes as structural elements of words.

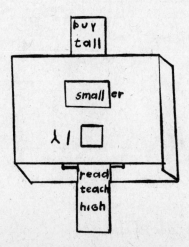

Activity:	Independent.
Materials:	Strips of tagboard or heavy paper, shallow boxes or lids.
Procedure:	Shallow boxes or lids of boxes can be made into tachistoscopes through which strips of tagboard or heavy paper can be pulled as the student pronounces the word with the prefix or suffix added. You can use two different prefixes or suffixes with the same box by turning it around and using another wordlist.

Title:	**"Affix Bingo"**
Purpose:	To help students recognize prefixes and suffixes quickly.
Activity:	Game.
Materials:	Bingo cards or dittoed sheets containing roots, prefixes, and suffixes.
Procedure:	Place five root words across the top of card. In squares below, write a *prefix* or *suffix* or *both*. When the caller says "Conduct," a player looks under "duct" to find the prefix "con" and marks that square. If "conductor" were called, he would have to find "con" and "or" before claiming the word. New cards can be made as soon as the class appears to have mastered one set.

arm	duct	vent	miss	test
-ful	con-	in-	-ion	-able
-y	in-		dis-	-ing
-ory	con- -or	ad- -ion con-	ad- -ion	re-
-ament	pro-	pre- -ed	-ing	de- -ing

Title:	**"Change Over"**
Purpose:	Word analysis drill on initial consonants, blends, and endings.

| *Materials:* | Cards of 3 x 5 inches with words printed on them: |

hat	shell	will	all	sing	sand	look
cat	will	spill	tall	wing	band	book
rat	fell	fill	wall	swing	land	brook
sat	tell	bill	ball	bring	hand	shook

Also four cards having these words: "change over."

| *Procedure:* | Deal out five cards. The child to the left of dealer plays any card, naming it. Next player either plays a card that rhymes or begins with the same letter. If the child cannot play, he draws from the extra cards until he can play or has drawn three cards. If he draws a "change over" card, he may play that and name a word that can be played upon. The first person out of cards wins the game. |

Title:	**"Syllables"**
Purpose:	To develop students' skill in dividing words into syllables.
Activity:	Game.
Materials:	Letters on cards.
Procedure:	Take a spelling word and write each letter on a separate card. (The bigger the cards the better.) Make black lines on cards which students will hold as a dividing line when necessary. The letters to the word are given at random to as many students as needed to make up that word. The teacher says the word and the students with the letters arrange themselves correctly by putting the letters on each side of the line as they are supposed to be.

For example: The teacher passes out letters for the word DEMAND. The teacher then says: "Our word is demand." The students arrange themselves correctly on either side of the dividing line. The teacher asks the rest of the group if the letter people have divided themselves correctly. If not, then a student comes to the front and rearranges the letters in the correct order.

Sample words for a lesson might be:
deserve, admirer, advantageous, accord, collision.

Provide a classroom chart with the following rules for syllabification

SYLLABIFICATION RULES

1. If a word has only one syllable, it cannot be divided.

   should   goat   book   have   light

2. A word which contains a double consonant usually should be divided between the double consonants.

   mut/ter   wig/gle   lap/ping   ad/dition

3. Compound words should be divided between the two smaller words.

   high/way   side/walk   fire/side

4. When a word contains a prefix or suffix, divide after the prefix or before the suffix.

   un/til   re/turn   sad/ness   play/ful

5. If two unlike consonants are between two vowels, divide between the consonants.

   mon/key   ser/vant   ig/nite

6. If a single consonant falls between two vowels, divide after the first vowel or consonant.

   cam/el   ti/ger   li/ly   bro/ken   py/thon

7. If the final syllable ends in le, the consonant before the le is usually included in the final syllable.

   cra/dle   sta/ble   bri/dle   ea/gle

Digraphs (kn, gn, th) and blends (fl, sl, tr) are treated as single letters.

   en/trance   al/though   tre/men/dous   un/known

Title:	**"Relay"**
Purpose:	To give practice in adding suffixes.
Activity:	Game.
Materials:	Develop four or five lists of words for adding suffixes with the suffix to be added at the top. Make each in duplicate—one for each group or row of students.
Procedure:	Give a list to each row or group. On "Go," the first student rewrites word adding suffix and passes it to the next student who does the next word and so on until each row or group finishes. The first row or group to finish with suffixes added correctly wins.

```
Add  ly

Happy
Quiet
Glad
Quick
```

PHONICS

Title: **"Phonic Wheel"**

Purpose: To recognize words through emphasis on the beginning consonants, consonant blends, or consonant diagraphs.

Activity: Independent.

Procedure: The wheel is made of two concentric circles fastened by a brass fastener through a hole punched in the center of the circles. As the pupil rotates the outer circle, he names the words that are formed by a combination of the beginning sound on the smaller wheel and the endings of words on the larger wheel.

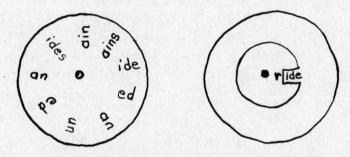

Variation: Ending used with different consonants.

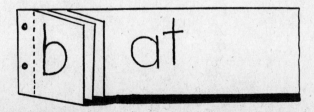

Title: **"Consonant Blends and Digraphs"**

Purpose.   To drill and reinforce the skill of differentiating sounds
                      and recognizing consonant blends and digraphs.

Activity: Class or small group.

Materials: 2 stacks of cards—1 containing words with consonant
                      blends—*blue*—the other with words containing
                      digraphs—*wh*ite.
                      small bulletin board and push pins.

Procedure: Choose 8 cards from each stack, mix them up and place
                      them face down on the board with a pin in each one. Let a
                      child choose 2 cards. The teacher turns them over and the
                      student decides if they match and tells if it is a blend or a
                      digraph. A ''match'' is either 2 consonant blends or 2
                      digraphs. These 16 cards can be replaced or remixed
                      from the 2 stacks from time to time.

	1	2	3	4
A				
B				
C				
D				

Call 1-A and 4-C. If a ''match'' is made, these two cards are removed from the board and the child calls two more numbers. He continues to call numbers as long as they match.

Blends: *bl*ue, *cl*own, *fl*ower, *gl*ove, *pl*an, *sl*eep, *spl*ice, *br*ead, *cr*ack, *dr*um, *fr*eeze, *gr*een, *pr*etty, *tr*ee, *thr*ow, *sc*ar, *sk*ate, *sm*oke, *sn*ail, *sp*ill, *st*ill, *sw*im, *scr*ape

Digraphs: *wh*ite, *ch*air, *th*is, *th*ink, *sh*oe, si*ng*, *th*eir, *th*em, *ch*aracter, *ch*ef, *ch*iffon, *ph*one, *Ph*ilip, ele*ph*ant, lau*gh*, cou*gh*, enou*gh*, ni*ck*el, du*ck*.

Title:	**"Matching Game"**
Purpose:	To provide practice in identifying initial consonant sounds.
Activity:	Individual or group.
Material:	Bulletin board, pictures of objects: letters, combination of letters.
Procedure:	Divide bulletin board into sections, each with a different letter or letters. Place in a pocket below. Student selects a picture and thumbtacks in section under correct letter which matches the initial sound of the word that the picture represents.

d	ch	sp	f
ch	k	m	n

pictures

Title:	**"Digraph Puzzle"**
Purpose:	To teach digraphs.
Activity:	Independent.
Procedure:	Reproduce the illustration below, along with the corresponding statements. Include directions that each statement should be read and the blank filled in with the appropriate word. Each word's digraph should be placed in the puzzle. On completion, students may want to make up their own puzzles.

1. A mouse likes to eat _____ .
2. A sailboat is a _____ .
3. The number after two is _____ .
4. Under my mouth is my _____ .
5. A car has four _____ .

1.		e	e	s	e
	2.		i	p	
3.		r	e	e	
		4.		i	n
5.		e	e	l	s

Title:	**"Prove It"**
Purpose:	To teach the student long and short vowel sounds.
Activity:	Group game.
Materials:	Flash cards.
Procedure:	The teacher flashes a card to a student in the class containing a word such as "cat." The student must read the word and tell whether it is a short or long "A" sound. When the student gives his answer, the teacher says, "Prove It." The student must then say the key word for the short "A" sound and repeat the word "cat." Such as "hat—cat."

Title:	**"Phonics Bingo"**
Purpose:	Students will match sounds and blends with pictures or letters.
Activity:	Group game
Materials:	Cardboard or posterboard. Pictures. Flash cards. Blends. Cover slips.

Procedure: Pass out bingo cards with pictures pasted on. Hold up flash card. If students have matching blends, they cover their cards' blend pictures. Whoever gets a row any way wins.

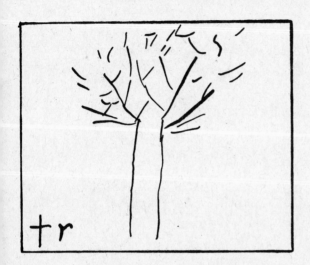

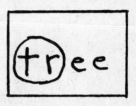

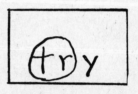

Title: **"Long or Short?"**

Purpose: To give children practice in recognizing long and short vowel sounds in words. It can be used for beginning, ending, or middle vowel sounds.

Activity: Whole class, small group, or individual.

Materials: Two posters, word cards.

Procedure: Have two posters, one of a Dachshund, the other of a Chihuahua, or any animals that would symbolize long and short. Each poster should have a pocket in which the child can insert the word cards. Stack the word cards in front of the posters. If used with a group, children should separate into groups or teams and take turns choosing a card, saying the word and putting it into the right pocket. One point is given for correct response.

If used independently, child should take all the word cards and read each, then put it in the correct pocket. The teacher can then check the cards or give students a list of long and short vowels for student to check with words in the poster.

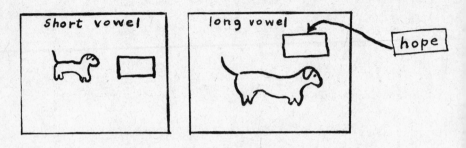

Title:	"Blend Finder Club"
Purpose:	The basic purpose of this activity is to help students recognize consonants in words, while at the same time they are learning new words.
Activity:	Group.
Materials:	A long sheet of wrapping paper or posterboard.
Procedure:	Title the paper "Blend Finders Club." Divide the sheet into columns, titling each column with a consonant blend. Tell the class you are starting a new club and to join they must find words containing blends. The students may find words from any source (text, library books, reference books, etc.) Each word can be recorded only once and you must be able to pronounce any word you write. When students find a word, they write it on the sheet under the proper blend and put their name beside the word, this makes them a member of the club.

Title:	"Consonant Blend Bingo"
Purpose:	To give practice in identifying consonant blends in the initial part of the key word.
Activity:	Group.
Materials:	Bingo card, tabs to cover cards, and call sheet.
Procedure:	Caller says key word. Student must cover the blend on his card that the key word begins with. Follow standard bingo rules.

Variations: Use also to practice other phonic skills; Example—write words in the squares, and ask student to cover word with long 0, etc.

tw	pr	pl	fr	tr
sp	str	dr	sm	bl
cl	gr	free	sc	spl
dw	cr	br	thr	sn
squ	spr	st	sw	scr

Title:	**"Turtle Race"**
Purpose:	To use team competition to check how well pupils know blends.
Activity:	Group.
Materials:	Large piece of paper or poster board. Construction paper. Cards (index).
Procedure:	Have blends written on cards with words the pupils have used. Example: spl—*Spl*ash
	Have them divide into two teams. Have two turtles cut out of construction paper and numbered 1 and 2. Pupils take turns reading the blend cards and if they read them

correctly they get to move their team's turtle one space.
The first turtle to the finish line wins.

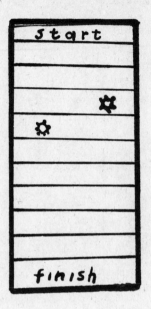

DICTIONARY SKILLS

Title:	**"Hop, Skip, and Jump"**
Purpose:	To give students practice in using dictionary skills.
Activity:	Game.
Procedure:	Write a list of 20 new words on the board.

Explain to the children that they are to copy the list,
locate each word in the dictionary, and write the dictionary pronunciation clues next to each word on their list.
Explain that after they have finished this assignment they
will play a game and will need to know how to pronounce
the words in order to play.

To play the game, divide your group into two teams.

Write one of the words on the blackboard and indicate
which child from each team is "up."

These two children should stand at a designated spot across the room from the blackboard. Tell them how to approach the board. Should they walk, skip, hop, walk backwards or what.

At the signal "go" the children race to the board in the designated manner, write the dictionary clues to pronunciation on the board. The child may use his paper.

The first child to finish is given the opportunity to pronounce the word. To be considered finished, the child must have written the pronunciation clues correctly, placed the chalk on the chalk railing, and be turned around facing the class. If the child pronounces the word correctly, he is the winner for that round, and his team makes one point. If he does not pronounce it correctly, the other child gets an opportunity to pronounce it. If he does so correctly, he makes a point for his team. If both children mispronounce the word, no one gets a point. See if anyone in the class can pronounce it. If both children misspell the word or "finish" at the same time, give them another word.

Continue in this manner until each child has had a turn. The team with the most points wins.

Title:	**"Opposites Puzzle"**
Purpose:	To provide dictionary practice in finding word meanings.
Activity:	Independent.
Procedure:	Recognizing words and using the dictionary are two skills which children need to develop. The puzzle on the following page helps do both. It is a puzzle using antonyms of the clues for answers. The words are simple, but in using opposites, it presents more of a challenge to the child. He may have to find two or three antonyms before one will fit properly.
	The complete puzzle follows but the puzzle as the children will receive it, appears following along with the clues.

Opposites!

Fill in the puzzle with opposites of the words below.
Clues

Across	Down
1. dumb	1. sit
3. hate	2. asleep
6. together	4. familiar
8. wet	5. begin
10. shallow	7. from
13. hot	9. floor
14. happy	11. hard
16. substract	12. bad
18. new	15. night
19. far	17. against

Title:	**"Dictionary Word Hunt"**
Purpose:	To develop skill in using the dictionary pronunciation key.
Activity:	Group.
Materials:	Dictionaries.
Procedure:	Teacher gives page number and definition of word, stu-

dents locate that word, and use pronunciation guide to enable them to pronounce the word. (Use words with which the students are unfamiliar.)

Title:	**"Guide Words Race"**
Purpose:	To enable students to classify words under correct guide words.
Activity:	Game.
Materials:	Flannelboard.
Procedure:	Divide class or group into two teams. Place guide words and ten words on flannelboard. First person on either team to correctly classify every word under the guide words gets a point for his team.

```
┌─────────────────────────────────────────────┐
│              ca  -  cr                        │
│  cement     happy        had                  │
│  civil      cave         crane                │
│  devil      creed        czar                 │
│  oral       cine         cope                 │
└─────────────────────────────────────────────┘
```

Title:	**"Dictionary Skills"**
Procedure:	This game can be played with children using an old game board. Make up cards with words for children to locate in the dictionary. On each card include a number, according to the difficulty of the word, that would indicate how many spaces to move when the word is found. Dice may be rolled to establish how many spaces to move. In order to move forward, the student must draw a word and look it up in the dictionary. Time limitations should be established as the players should only be allowed a certain

amount of time commensurate with their ability. If a
player finds the word in the alloted time, he may read the
definition and then move the specified number of spaces
on either the word card or on the dice. If he does not find
the word, he must move backward the number on the
word card and the card goes back into the pile.

This may be more competitive with teams racing against
each other to find the word first.

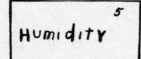

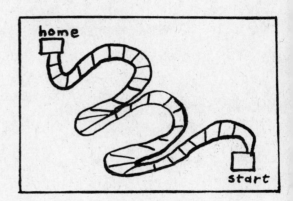

VOCABULARY RELATIONSHIPS

Title:	**"Dominoes"**
Purpose:	To learn meanings of homonyms and antonyms.
Activity:	Game.
Materials:	Pieces of poster board. If the game is to be played with a group, the size of the cards should be no less than 5 x 7. Large cards are easy to see.
Procedure:	An explanation of how cards may be placed is necessary. Also a brief explanation of antonyms and homonyms is wise. If the game is being played with a group, it would be necessary to divide the group into two teams. A playing space of 10′ to 12′ is needed. Each team is to place its domino cards in the correct order. When each team has finished placing its cards, they should cross-check each other's work.

far	day
near	

go	stop	night

pair	mail
pear	

see	sea	male

Title:	**"Compound Word Hunt"**
Purpose:	To introduce compound words.
Activity:	Independent.
Materials:	Ditto with illustrations representing compound words.
Procedure:	Tell a student that if he will say the names of the two pictures in a row he will hear a new word (compound word). If he can spell each word separately, he can spell the compound word by putting the two together.

  = fishhook

 = treehouse

Title:	**"Antonyms and Synonyms"**
Purpose:	Recognition of antonyms and synonyms.
Materials:	Flash cards with antonyms and synonyms
Procedure:	Write the following words on board:

        behind   same

        tell   black

miserable	stolen
scream	least
silently	hurriedly
spoiled	aid

Divide class into team A and team B. Flash cards will have either a synonym or an antonym for a word written on the board. Flash a word to first member of team A. He must either say whether the word is a synonym or an antonym. If team A misses, team B has a turn. Continue flashing words to alternating sides until correct answer is obtained. Right answer gets one point. Team with most points wins.

Title:	**"Password"**
Purpose:	To learn to recognize antonyms.
Activity:	Game.
Procedure:	A caller is chosen for each team for the first word. He is shown the word written on a slip of paper along with the caller for the other team. He calls out a word that has the opposite meaning as a clue to his partner. If his partner guesses what the word is, their team scores ten points. If they do not get it correctly on the first try, the second caller gives his partner a clue of opposite meaning. If the second team guesses correctly, they score nine points. They continue back and forth until the word is worth only one point. The team that scores 50 points wins. The caller and partner switch roles every word.

Title:	**"Antonyms and Homonyms"**
Purpose:	To learn word relationships of antonyms and homonyms.
Materials:	Overhead Transparency—already prepared. Dittos
Procedure:	1. Go over orally with the children the transparency which contains these sentences:

"*Smell* is to *nose* just as *hear* is to _____

"*Glad* is to *sorry* just as *pull* is to _____

"*One* is to *first* just as *three* is to _____

"*Door* is to *house* just as *gate* is to _____

"*Sing* is to *song* just as *leave* is to _____

"*Bread is to flour* just as *wagon* is to _____

2. Let the children respond when they come up with the correct answer and let one write in the block.

3. After you feel they follow relationships, give them a ditto - Example:

Sea is to *see* as *him* is to _____

Women is to *lady* as *boy* is to _____

Cool is to *warm* as *empty* is to _____

Whisper is to *shout* as *outside* is to _____

Forget is to *remember* as *sold* is to _____

For those who finish early, introduce them to a card game—"Authors" root words—suffixes and prefixes.

52 cards total—4 cards in a book. Object is to collect books. Game is played like "Fish."

ROOT WORD IS WASH

wash	washed
wash	wash
washed	washed
washes	washes
washing	washing

washes	washing
wash	wash
washed	washed
washes	washes
washing	washing

(all four cards equal one book)

Examples of other root words: teach, count, like, play, add

Title:	**"Homonym Drill"**
Purpose:	To help students develop the ability to recognize homonyms.
Materials:	5 x 8 cards with homonyms written on different cards.
Procedure.	Explain the game:

A. Each student will receive one card which has two words written thereon.

B. The teacher will begin the drill by pronouncing a word and using it in a sentence.

C. The student who has the card with the homonym of the word used by the teacher will stand, pronounce the word, and use it in a sentence. The student will then pronounce the second word on his card and use it in a sentence.

D. The drill will then continue with the students following the procedure as stated in above.

Title:	**"Letters Make Words"**
Activity:	Group.
Procedure:	The object of the game is to fill in a 36-block diagram with as many 6-letter words as possible. The words can be spelled horizontally, vertically, and diagonally. Only 6-letter words count diagonally so it is best to start with them. All 6-letter words count 20 points. 5-letters—10 points; 4 letters—5 points; 3 letters—2 points. (If the teacher feels that having only 6-letter words count diagonally makes the game too complicated for her students, this rule can be deleted.
	To begin play, one student calls out a letter and each member of the class must write the letter in his diagram; or if he wishes, the letter can be put in stand-by until he decides its best use. Only one letter can be in stand-by at one time. Play proceeds with each student calling out a letter until 36 letters have been called.
Purpose:	Aside from just having fun with words, students are using spelling skills and learning new words. They must also use planning and organizing skills. Since the longer

words count more than shorter ones, they will find themselves searching for new 6-letter words. For most groups,
it would be advisable to have the students plan ahead so
they will have some words in mind and will not just put
the letters in at random.

	1	2	3	4	5	6
13 7	B	A	K	E	R	M
8	E	E	R	B	O	A
9	T	R	A	D	A	R
10	T	G	N	U	S	S
11	E	A	W	I	T	H
12 14	R	E	A	L	T	Y

Row Number	No. of Letters	Points	Word
1	6	20	Better
2	-	0	-
3	3	2	Ran
4	-	0	-
5	5	10	Roast
6	6	20	Marshy
7	5	10	Baker
8	3	2	Boa
9	5	10	Radar
10	3	2	Gnu
11	4	5	With
12	6	20	Realty
13	6	20	Beauty
14	6	20	Random

Total   141

Title:	**"Meanings Within Meanings"**
Purpose:	To make children aware that synonyms can be used interchangeably.
Activity:	Group or independent.
Materials:	Dictionaries and Webster's Dictionary of Synonyms.
Procedure:	On a dictionary discovery day, give your students a simple word as "foam" to look up. Add to their findings synonyms from a dictionary of synonyms. In some words, students may discover that each synonym has a slightly different meaning. Connotations are hard for anyone to discover for himself. Keep one spot on the board for words students ask about, then assign them to word scouts to trace down in extra time.
Illustration:	1. Foam—liquid topping having small bubbles. 2. Scum—film that comes on top of liquids. 3. Spume—liquid from agitated water. 4. Froth—both foam and frills. 5. Lather and suds—soapy foam.

Title:	**"Compound Words Tic - Tac - Toe"**
Purpose:	To provide drill on compound words.
Activity:	Group.
Materials:	Paper, chalkboard, compound words.
Procedure:	The first part of a compound word is printed on paper used as flashcard. The second part is printed on chalkboard. Divide the class into two equal teams. If there is one player left over, he could become the card-flasher. A card is shown to the first person on team X. If a correct combination is made, an X is put in the square with the word on the board. The idea is to get a row of X's or 0's vertically, horizontally, or diagnonally. If no pattern is established, the team with the most symbols wins.

DRAW	BOARD	GET	WALK	WRECK
BIRD	FALL	BOX	FOOT	PROOF
SHINE	SIDE	**SPREAD**	HOOD	SPOON
WORK	FIRE	MOTHER	FLY	NAIL
PORT	BOOK	PASTE	STICK	SMITH

Improving Reading Competency with Comprehension Skill Development Through 34 Activities

Everyone who teaches reading realizes that having students comprehend what they read is the real goal. The means to this end is the teaching of many skills to students so that they will be able to understand fully what the author is trying to convey. Therefore, we teach the word recognition skills and the comprehension skills which relate to the skill of reading. In the previous chapter, activities were provided for word recognition skill development and in this chapter activities are provided for comprehension skill development.

Comprehension is a generalized reading skill which is composed of several sub-skills. Reading authorities tend to agree that systematic instruction of the comprehension sub-skills will help your students become good comprehenders. With this in mind, that direct instruction of the comprehension sub-skills will lead to better reading comprehension, this chapter has been organized and divided into six sub-sections: general comprehension, main ideas, understanding sequence and sentence building, reading for details and skimming, study skills, and critical reading. Again, each sub-section contains ideas for games, group and independent activities.

Every experienced teacher knows that children need not only to learn reading skills, but to overlearn these skills so they will become permanent skills. Without sufficient instruction and practice, children tend to forget the skills taught from any reading program. No reading program contains sufficient skill instruction to meet the needs of all students, making it imperative that each teacher provide additional instruction to those students who need heavier than usual dosage. Here is where these activities play a vital role in your reading program. For these detailed experiences will enable you to teach with precision, thereby providing sufficient instructioned dosage to every student who has observable skill needs.

GENERAL COMPREHENSION

Title:　　　**"Flower Power"**

Purpose:　　To develop comprehension skills.

Activity:　　Group game.

Procedure:　On 3″ x 5″ index cards write a word and its synonym in different colors. For example:

molasses (red)	syrup (blue)

Definition:　A thick, sweet liquid made by boiling sugar with water.

Give each student one card. Those students with red cards belong to the Red Flower team, and those students with blue cards, belong to the Blue Flower team. The teacher or leader reads one definition for which there are two answers, or synonyms. The first student to hold up his card with the correct synonym wins a point for his team. Points will be shown by adding a petal to the team's flower. The first team to complete its flower by having all ten petals up wins the game.

Red Flower Team

Blue Flower Team

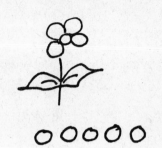

Title:	**"Comprehension Spinner"**
Purpose:	To develop remembering power.
Activity:	Game.
Procedure:	Have the class read a story silently; then tell them there will now be a game. Point out that this game will be used in the future so they should read very carefully.

Divide the class into two teams and spin the dial—where it lands will be the question the first team must answer correctly. If the team answers correctly then score one point. If the team answers incorrectly, then give the question to the next team. If the second team answers it correctly, then they also get the next question since the first question was not really supposed to be theirs. Score two points if they answer the other team's question correctly and one point if they answer their own question. If the second team can answer only "their" question, then again score for them only one point and give the unanswered question to the opposite team and so on. After all questions on the board have been answered correctly, the team with the highest score wins.

The round board with questions on it can be made out of plywood or poster board. It can be on the bulletin board or set in front of the room. The teacher can turn the dial.

Questions on the board can be used for any story the class would read.

Questions to be written on the board are: Where did the story take place? What was the name of the story? How were the people dressed? Were there any animals in the story? What happened in the story? Did the story have a happy ending? Who were the main characters in the story? What time of year do you think this story took place? What was the most exciting part of the story? (Of course there are still others that could be written on the board depending on the side of the board and the questions asked).

Have each section of the board painted a different color. The dial can be made out of a piece of board or cardboard with the point glued on.

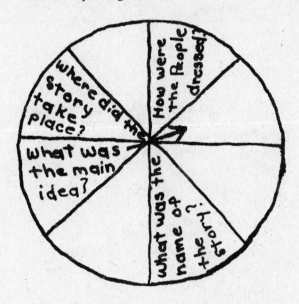

Title:	**"Crossword Delight"**
Purpose:	To check comprehension.
Activity:	Independent.
Procedure:	A crossword puzzle can be used to determine a student's

comprehension of a story or his knowledge of new vocabulary.

ACROSS

1. Tom used John's _____ to get air.
7. Linda got a piece of coral in her _____ .
8. "Word used to express a choice."
9. The name of John's sister.
10. The boys went diving in the Florida _____ .
12. How many boys were there?
14. Opposite of he.
15. There was only _____ girl.
16. Golfers use this to tee off.
17. The ship was _____ .
19. The boys brought some of the treasure _____ board ship.

DOWN

2. Their tanks were filled with _____ .
3. Who sank the ship?
4. Give the abbrev. for the state John and Linda were from.
5. What was their first piece of treasure?
6. The ship was hidden in a _____ .
10. The island the boys wanted to visit.
11. Opposite of no.
13. Linda was so scared of the Beardman that she _____ .
14. Their largest treasure was an old _____ .
18. Opposite of she.

Title: **"Mural Game"**

Purpose: To teach students to remember what they have read.

Activity: Group.

Procedure: Have a small group read an assigned story, but before they read tell them that they are going to play a game afterwards about the characters and the background in the story; so they should remember as many details as they can.

After the students read, have them put the story material away. Using the blackboard or paper, tell them that each one is to make part of a mural. Assign characters and one by one have them draw the character or object and tell about it. (e.g. I'm Janet; I have yellow hair; and I run in the story. Or, I'm a tree; I move in the wind; and I'm old and tall.) For each item they can tell they get a point. The winner is the one with the most points.

Title: **"Story Box Questions"**

Purpose: To develop comprehension skills.

Activity: Group.

Procedure: Make a decorated story box with questions on index cards about the story the class read. Give each child a turn. Those that miss can be reminded to read more carefully next time or be given another chance after everyone else has had one chance. Go around the room and let each child select a card without first looking at it. Give the class a few minutes to get ready and then ask each child to read his question and give the answer. There should be as many questions as there are children with only slight overlapping of answers.

Some of the questions in your story box can be: What did you like best about the story? What would you have done in the same situation? Which character did you like best? Would you like to be in that story? Did the children have on winter clothes? Were the children in the story about your age? What part of the story did you like best? Was there a mother and a father in the story? Were there any pets in the story? How many people were in the story? Did the story take place in the city or the country? What happened in the story? What were the names of the characters in the story? Do you like to read this kind of story—if so why? Was it a happy story? Were there any new words in the story? What was the first thing that happened in the story? How did the story end?

MAIN IDEAS

Title:	**"What Is It All About?"**
Purpose:	To give students practice in the questioning skills necessary in finding main ideas of reading materials.
Activity:	Group or independent.
Materials:	Ditto sheet or sentences written on chalkboard.
Procedure:	The main ideas of reading material can be found by asking the questions When?, What?, Why?, and How? This exercise will give students practice that can later be applied to reading text or independent materials. Give students ditto sheets with sentences which will answer one of the above questions (When?, What?, Why?, How?). They will read each sentence and tell which question it answers and what part of the sentence answers the question.
Example:	*He was afraid*, so he ran away. *Why?*

Title:	**"Choose a Name"**
Purpose:	To provide practice in classification and getting main idea of a paragraph.
Activity:	Group.
Materials:	Paragraphs written on dittos. Title on back for self-correction. Titles on small cards. Three different titles for each story.

Procedure: Pass out sheets to students. They read paragraphs and then decide on the best title. They can read silently, choose title, then read aloud and discuss the titles.

Illustration: "Petunia, the duck, loved to swim. She would swim all day if she could. Then when she was tired, she would take one last swim home. She always had busy days."

Choices: 1. "A Day at the Lake."
2. "The Duck Who Loved to Swim."
3. "Ducks and Water."

Title: **"Search and Find"**

Purpose.   To give students practice in determining the main idea of a paragraph.

Activity   This is a bulletin board activity to be used first with the class as a whole; then individual students can manipulate the bulletin board independently. Each student is allowed to participate actively in this bulletin board experience.

Materials: Bulletin board, (or wall space), paper, construction paper, envelope

Procedure: First, write several short paragraphs on paper, and mount the paragraphs on construction paper. Attach the construction paper to the bulletin board. Write a title for each paragraph on strips of paper, and place the strips in an envelope mounted on the bulletin board. Include a few extra titles which do not fit the paragraphs. Have the students take turns in matching the correct titles with the correct paragraphs. After the students are able to do this on their own, instruct each student to make up a paragraph and the best title. This activity can be stretched out over a long period of time by mounting several paragraphs at a time.

UNDERSTANDING SEQUENCE AND SENTENCE BUILDING

Title: **"Spin-a-Sentence"**

Purpose: Sentence buildings.

Activity: Game.

Procedure: This game is played by a group of six. The group is divided up into two teams. A numbered spin wheel is used and each team is given a numbered list of words. The object of the game is for a team to spin a number and using the corresponding numbered word use it to build a sentence. Each team takes one word at a time until the first team to make a complete sentence wins.

Note: If a team spins a number already used, this constitutes a turn played.

Title: **"Wheel Game"**

Purpose: This game will help build vocabulary, sentence building, and paragraph structure.

Activity: Game.

Procedure: Make a large cardboard clockface, numbered from 1 to 12, or more or less. Put a hand on it fastened by a large fastener.

On a ditto sheet, make three different lists of words, numbered same as clock. Divide class into three groups.

List of Words
1. Carol
2. went
3. something
4. toy
5. read
6. picture
7. sleep
8. play
9. winter
10. stop
11. large
12. home

Spin the hand, then wherever it lands say, "2," have a child from group 1 say the word on his paper for #2 and then use it in a sentence. Write it on the board. Do this again, each group taking a turn. Go back to group 1 and when they get the second word, the sentence they make up has to relate to the first sentence. If a child doesn't know the word, or can't think of a sentence, that group forfeits its turn. The first group with a completely related paragraph wins.

Title:	**"Combining Sentences"**
Purpose:	To help students build complex sentences by combining given sets of three simple sentences.
Activity:	Independent.
Materials:	Printed copies containing sets of three simple sentences about one subject.
Procedure:	Instruct student to combine each set of sentences to form one longer, more descriptive sentence. Use the first set as an example.
Example:	Sixth Grade

SET I
1) We have a big, white horse.
2) He lives on our farm.
3) He can run as fast as the wind.

Possible solution: On our farm, we have a big, white horse that can run as fast as the wind.

SET II
1) Today we went on a field trip.
2) We found a black snake.
3) It was eighteen inches long.

Sentence: _____

SET III
1) Mr. Ray has a sixth-grade class.
2) There are 36 students in his class.
3) Twenty students are boys and 16 students are girls.

Sentence: _____

SET IV   1) I am a girl (boy).
                2) I have brown (blond) hair and brown (blue) eyes.
                3) I am 11 (12) years old.

Sentence: _____

SET V   1) I missed school yesterday.
              2) I had a bad cold.
              3) My mother made me stay in bed.

Sentence: _____

Title: **"Stop and Go"**

Purpose: To help the student become more proficient in his oral reading and to aid in the sequential following of the passage by the group participants.

Materials: Books (possibly the Reader), chairs or individual rugs, stop watch, rewards or prizes.

Activity: Small group.

Procedure: The students should sit in a semi-circle with the teacher seated at the front serving as proctor. A reading passage is assigned with a student reading until one of his peers notices a reading error such as mispronouncing a word, stuttering, etc. The student who recognized the mistake corrects it and reads until he is stopped. This continues till the story is completed. The student who reads the longest without being corrected wins a prize. If a reading error goes unnoticed by the students, the teacher corrects the mistake then appoints another student to read.

            The group size will depend upon the passage being read and the reading level of the students. For effectiveness it should not go beyond ten children.

Title: **"Taping of Oral Reading"**

Purpose: To motivate students in a type of "Look-Say" situation to read and listen to themselves reading. (Children like to use the tape recorder. It has built-in motivation.)

Activity: Group or independent.

Materials:
1. Preselected poem preferably long enough to give students adequate reading time and challenging enough to make them learn new words. A story could also be used.
2. Tape recorder
3. Enough books for every student

Procedure:
1. Select a poem.
2. Number of lines in poem are counted so that each student has approximately the same number of lines.
3. Each student is then assigned his lines and allotted about 5 minutes or so for practice.
4. Each student then reads his lines with next student ready in order to avoid lapses and give unity to poem. Teacher can move microphone close in order to avoid moving around by students and students should be gathered around close enough also to avoid movement during recording.
5. When finished, the entire recording is then played back.
6. Follow-up discussion on contents or the ideas of the poem should of course be utilized.

Title: **"Cut Ups"**

Purpose: To help students develop the ability to arrange a story in sequence.

Materials: Envelopes with sentences to make a story.

Procedure: Give each student an envelope and give them time to arrange their stories in correct order. They can be checked by answering cards or read orally to the class so errors can be discussed.

Illustration.   Cut up sentences and put in envelope.

1. On Monday Kevin had to wash his dog Muff.

    2. First he got out some soap and water in a tub.

    3. Muff didn't like to be washed, so next Kevin had to catch him.

    4. Finally he got Muff in the tub and wet him.

    5. After that he rubbed him all over with soap and then rinsed him.

    6. When Kevin was done he got out of the way so Muff could shake.

Title:	**"Sequencing a Class Experience Story"**
Purpose:	To develop students' ability to understand story sequence.
Activity:	Group.
Materials:	1. Experience story on chart paper.
	2. Story reproduced on ditto paper.
	3. Scissors
	4. Construction paper
	5. Paste
Procedure:	1. The students reread orally the story which the class at large composed the previous day.
	2. Put emphasis on the fact that the story covered the events of dyeing eggs in the order in which the egg-dyeing procedure occurred.
	3. Give students a scrambled copy of the chart story.
	4. Each student first numbers the sentences in the proper sequential order.
	5. Then each student cuts out the individual story sentences and pastes them in proper order on construction paper.
	6. Each student will give his own title to the story.

Illustration:

SEQUENTIAL ORDER

Today we all brought in three eggs.

The eggs were hard-boiled at home.

We colored our eggs at school.

First we filled ten cups with water.

Then we put some dye in each cup.

We had four colors to choose from.

The colors were red, yellow, blue, and green.

Next we added vinegar to the colored water.

Then we dipped our eggs in the water to dye them.

Some people dipped the eggs in two and three colors

The colored eggs are Easter eggs.

We are going to have an Easter egg hunt tomorrow

We are also going to have a party.

We can't wait!

READING FOR DETAILS AND SKIMMING

Title:	**"Skimming the Newspaper"**
Purpose:	To provide practice in skimming.
Activity:	Group.
Materials:	Old newspapers. Ditto list of instruction.
Procedure:	Give each child a newspaper. Give each child a list of things to find.
Example:	1. Find a date.
	2. Find the name of a country.
	3. Find the name of a person.
	4. Find an item used in cleaning.
	5. Find someone's age.
	6. Find a time.
	7. Find a price.

Many items can be added to this list. This activity will also acquaint the child with the the many aspects of the newspaper.

Title:	**"Score Board Basketball"**
Purpose:	To develop the ability to skim for facts.
Activity:	Group.
Procedure:	Have children read material and skim it for facts, figures, dates, and ideas. Set a time limit of 90 seconds (your

option) on the game. They must answer questions by writing the answers down on a piece of paper and wadding it up and throwing it in a designated cardboard box. At the end of 90 seconds, a monitor will cover the box and let the teacher read the answers. Keep this up, making the material more difficult each time and try variations on the time limits.

Example: Ask the child questions about a story concerning Columbus coming to America. "When did Columbus start sailing for America?"

On slip of paper child writes the answer.

| 1492 |

Title: **"Sports Report"**

Purpose: To give students practice in scanning for details.

Activity: Independent.

Materials: Pages from the sports section of a recent newspaper. Small strips of paper.

Procedure: Capitalize on interest in sports. Cut the sports section of a current newspaper into separate pages. To each page attach a strip of paper on which you have written a question which can be answered by reading one of the articles on that page. *Do not* specify which article. The question may be factual or may require the student to draw a conclusion based on details in the article. The student will determine, by scanning, which article will probably contain the information he needs. He will then read the article for detail in order to locate the answer to his question. The student should share his answer with the class or with the group of boys participating in the activity.

Title: **"Find It Fast"**

Purpose: To develop skimming abilities of students.

Activity: Group game.

Procedure: Divide the class into two teams. Use the overhead projector to show the class a list of vocabulary words. Before showing them the list, tell the students to look for a particular kind of word; for example. "Look for something you can wear." (sweater).

Then flash the list on the screen for about three seconds. Ask if anyone on team I saw the correct word. If so, Team 1 gets a point. If they do not know the word, ask Team II.

An example list and questions might be the following:

watch	green
summer	kangaroo
sweater	potato

1. Look for something you can wear (sweater).
2. Look for something you can eat (potato).
3. Look for a word that is a color (green).
4. Look for a word that is a season (summer).
5. Look for an animal (kangaroo).
6. Look for something that tells you time (watch).

After flashing the list to the class the first three times, do not show it to them anymore. If students have completely forgotten all the words, you may show it to them once more quickly, but students should not take long to memorize most of the words after several times.

After mastering the words, the teacher could replace the list with a list of sentences. Then the questions might be directed to catching the most important word or words that finish the sentence. Later, paragraphs from stories they have read, or are preparing to read, may be used. Of course you will have to allow a little more time for the students to skim over the paragraphs. Teacher might ask for details or main ideas.

Title: **"Skimming to Bingo"**

Purpose: To provide skimming practice in locating a particular answer.

Activity: Group game.

Procedure: Each child is given an identical passage or story with sentences numbered, as well as a BINGO card such as below.

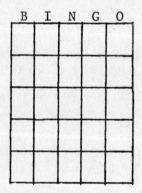

B   I   N   G   O

All squares of card should be numbered randomly from one to x (x being the number of sentences in the story); and no two cards should be alike.

Teacher prepares questions on article, writing each on a separate card to be randomly picked and read to children. Students skim article to find answer to each question, marking any block on the card corresponding to the number of the particular sentence. First child to have an entire row of five—horizontally, vertically, or diagonally—filled in is winner (BINGO!)

Title: **"What Do You Remember?"**

Purpose: To develop skill in remembering details.

Activity: Independent.

Materials: Handout of a detailed description.

Procedure: The teacher gives each student a copy of a detailed description of some very weird, far-out character. Instruct the students to read this carefully. Then tell them to return the descriptions. Tell the students to draw a picture of the character and put in as many details as they can remember reading about. Students then could show their products in small groups comparing the other members'.

Title:	**"Grasping Details"**
Purpose.	To give children a chance to find and compare details of stories.
Directions:	In the primary grades, the teacher reads very short stories to the class. They name the like and unlike details as a group, and the teacher lists them on the board. In the upper grades, the students can do this as an independent activity, reading the stories silently and recording their own list.
	Have two versions of a story or two similar stories.
	Have stories read (either by teacher or student); and after the students have heard or read each, they tell in written or oral form the things that are alike and different about the two stories. Be sure that students understand the directions and purpose before they start reading, or they may not know what to look for in the reading.

STUDY SKILLS

Title:	**"Categories"**
Purpose:	To encourage the use of a variety of reference works.
Activity:	Independent.
Materials:	A diagram dittoed on a sheet of paper, access to several reference materials.
Procedure:	A five letter word, like GAMES, is written at the top of the diagram. Words containing Q, Y, Z, or double letters should not be used. The horizontal rows should name large classifications such as rivers, cities, countries, famous people, etc. These are written on the left side. Then for row one, the pupil fills in rivers all the way across; row two, cities, etc.
	In scoring, give 5 points (for example) for an answer no

one else has; if 2 have the same answer, 3 points; 1 point for an answer three or more have. This correlates well with other subject areas.

	G	A	M	E	S
Rivers	Ganges	Amazon	Moselle	Elbe	Scheldt
Cities	Genoa	Athens	Moscow	Edinburgh	Stockholm
Countries	Germany	Arabia	Mexico	Egypt	Siam
Famous People	Grant	Adams	Monroe	Edison	Socrates
School Subjects	Geography	Arithmetic	Music	English	Science

Title: **"Locating Information in the Library"**

Purpose: To provide practice in developing library skills.

Activity: Group or independent.

Directions: Take the class on a trip to the library. Explain the different techniques used in libraries. Give the following practice exercise.

1. In which drawer of the card catalog would you look for a book by Laura Ingalls Wilder?
2. In which drawer of the card catalog would you look for the title of another book by the author of *A Snowy Day*?
3. Draw an author card, title card, and subject card.
4. Who is the author of *Kim*?
5. What is the call number of *Tom Sawyer*?
6. What books written by the author of *The Singing Tree* are in your library?
7. What is the title and call number in your library of a book on early pioneer life?

8. What facts, other than the title and author, are given on the subject for the book *Treasure Island*?
9. What else might you find on a card titled Thomas Edison?
10. Draw a diagram of the library and show where the books for the very young children are kept.
11. Show on your diagram where other books are kept.

CRITICAL READING

Title:	**"Friendly Persuasion"**
Purpose:	To help students become aware of what propaganda is and how it is used in advertising. To acquaint them with some of the terms applied to types of propaganda.
Activity:	Group.
Materials:	Slogans form advertisements on posterboard or chalkboard.
Procedure:	Display slogans, and discuss them. Find out how many agree with the advertising and why. Ask the students to question the "message" in each one to see if they can find fallacies in them. If possible, try to have them classify the slogans, (Glittering generalities, testimonial, bandwagon, etc.) Have them write a few commercial ads, or write *true* advertisements for products like cigarettes, telling it as it really is.
Illustration:	Brand X tastes better! (Better than what? Who says so?) If you use XY soap, your dishes will sparkle! (But will they be clean?) *True advertisement*: If you smoke CLEAN cigarettes, you will have bad breath, short wind, and die young.

Title:	**"Contest Advercology"**
Purpose:	To guide children to think critically about contests.
Activity:	Group.

Materials:	Several examples of contest ads taken from newspapers and magazines.
Procedure.	Ask children about types of contest they may have entered or heard about.
	Ask, "What type of rules were involved."
	Ask, "Why do companies have contests."
	Point out the examples of contest and explain what is involved in each of them . Discuss the merits of competition. Discusss possible bad effects of competition.
	Have children form groups to investigate selected contests. Have groups report their findings to the class either orally or in written form.

Title:	**"Fact-Opinion Cards"**
Purpose:	To provide practice in differentiating statements of fact or opinion.
Activity:	Group.
Materials:	Two cards for every child in group. One is marked FACT (in blue) and the other is marked OPINION (in red)
Procedure:	Give each student two cards, one red and one blue. Read selections from newspapers. When a fact comes up or an opinion is read, students hold up their card according to what they think it is. They must be able to justify why they are holding up that particular card if called on. Later on, let each student write a list of his own facts and opinions and read them to classmates.

Title:	**"Evaluating News Articles"**
Purpose:	To give students practice in evaluating news articles.
Activity:	Group.
Procedure:	Using a cardboard box, cut out a large square and draw circles making it look like a TV set. Instruct students to bring in articles from newspaper and while reading them,

act as a newscaster on TV. Have each student report the articles in his own words. Then have each reporter tell the class if his article is fact or opinion and bring out points the newspaper may have exaggerated.

Title:	**"Fact or Opinion?"**
Purpose:	To help students to differentiate between statements of FACT or OPINION.
Materials:	Two cards for every student with one marked FACT and the other OPINION.
Procedure:	Have children read a story silently. Have a list of statements from the story to be read to children. Have them hold up card—either FACT or OPINION. Challenge their answers.

Title:	**"Impostor"**
Purpose:	Distinguishing between fact or opinion.
Activity:	Group.
Materials:	Write the name of one of the characters on one side of an index card. On the reverse side, write several statements about the character using the second person. You may want to use characters from stories that have been read in class.
Procedure:	Give one student one of the cards. He then goes before the Judge and says "I am Alexander" (or whoever he is assigned). Then the Judge takes his card and reads each statement. The Character replies either Fact or Opinion. If he is correct, he replaces the Judge, and if he is wrong the Judge says "Impostor!" and he must go back to his

```
┌─────────────┐   ┌──────────────────────────────────────────┐
│  ALEXANDER  │   │ 1.  You lost your coat. (fact            │
└─────────────┘   │ 2.  You didn't like school. (opinion)    │
                  │ 3.  You had a dog named Tug. (fact)      │
                  │ 4.  You wished you had more              │
                  │     brothers and sisters. (opinion)      │
                  └──────────────────────────────────────────┘
```

seat. Then another student is chosen to be another character.

Title:	**"Real or Fanciful?"**
Purpose:	Develop critical thinking—fact or fiction
Activity:	Group.
Materials:	Good imaginations.
Procedure:	Invite the children to make up a story about the life of an imaginary character. Have one fanciful version, suggest words or phrases that are often used in fanciful stories (Once upon a time, killing dragons, super-human). After the fanciful version is written, write a real version of the story using the other as a model. Compare stories pointing out key fanciful words.

Title:	**"Fact-Fancy-Opinion"**
Purpose:	This exercise is designed to teach children to discriminate between factual reports, fanciful tales or opinion. Many students believe print has to be accurate, and they should have the ability to discriminate between these differences.
Activity:	Group or independent.
Materials:	Textbooks, pictures from magazines or prepared sentences.
Procedure:	If textbooks or magazines are used, have children decide whether or not characters could act the way they do, or show pictures to decide if they are fact or fancy. They should be able to give reasons for their answers.

Example: After reading a selection from the textbook, prepare appropriate sentences that apply to the story. Example could be similar to the following:

1. There are fairy godmothers who bring children gifts.
2. Some women think that men should never cry.
3. *The Crystal Flask* is the name of the book.
4. Some people think tears bring happiness.

Have children mark correct answer—i.e.

A. Fact
B. Fancy
C. Opinion.

Title:	**"Caution!"**
Purpose:	To help children develop critical reading abilities by alerting them to the use of false claims, exaggerated or omitted facts, glittering generalities, emotionalism, catch phrases and other such devices which are used in some mass media articles and advertisements for the purpose of persuading or influencing readers.
Activity:	Combination of independent and small group.
Materials:	Magazine or newspaper articles and advertisements which contain examples of the above devices.
	One large sheet of poster paper per group.
	Scissors, glue, one or two magic markers, construction paper (optional).
Procedure:	Explain to children that the best way to persuade a person is to present all the facts as honestly as possible, but sometimes writers use less acceptable devices such as exaggerated or omitted facts, catch phrases, false claims, glittering generalities, etc. in order to influence or persuade readers. Explain these various devices and show examples that you have clipped from newspapers and magazines.
	Over a period of time encourage children to look for examples and bring them to school. Keep them in a folder until they have collected enough for several posters. Then have children, in groups, make posters to display the examples. Glue the advertisements and articles on posterboard. Draw attention to the "offenders" by circling them with a bright-colored magic marker. Let children think up an appropriate heading for the poster such as Caution!, etc. Letters for the heading can be cut from construction paper or they can be applied directly to the poster with a magic marker.

Title:	**"Opinion—Yes or No"**
Purpose:	To provide corrective practice for pupils deficient in critical reading.
Activity:	Individual.
Procedure:	State that opinions are merely beliefs which cannot be supported by objective evidence, but that facts, on the contrary, are capable of being proved through objective evidence. Use statements such as:

1. Men make better legislators than women (opinion).
2. The majority of legislators are men (fact).
3. California oranges are better than Florida oranges (opinion).
4. Oranges contain Vitamin C (fact).

CHAPTER 11

25 Classroom Activities That

Insure Language Readiness

As you are aware, children vary widely in their readiness skills when they come to school entering kindergarten or first grade. The responsibility for teaching readiness skills is shared by kindergarten and first-grade teachers, and if you are one of them, you will find the interesting, readiness activities in this chapter of great help in meeting the skill needs of your children.

The readiness activities are classified and grouped by their categories enabling you to go directly to the activities pertaining to a certain skill. For example, the first group of activities relates to developing visual discrimination abilities of students followed by auditory discrimination instructional ideas, alphabet identification and order, and story sequence. Among each of these sub-groups are games, group and independent activities, to assist you in individualizing your instructional program.

Suppose your students need visual discrimination skill development. The first activity is "Surprise Squares!!!," a useful teaching idea for students to work on independently. For a group activity, you could select the second activity, "Mix and Match." Of course, many, if not all, group activities are fun, but should you want a game, you could select "Picture Word Lotto." Thus you have an array of creative ideas providing you with instructional versatility to make your instruction productive and exciting.

VISUAL DISCRIMINATION

Title:	**"Surprise Squares !"**
Purpose:	To learn visual discrimination.
Activity:	Independent.
Materials:	Ditto "Surprise Squares" Children color squares and come up with picture when they have discriminated correctly.
Procedure:	Ditto marked off in squares with basic sight words. Children are to color certain words certain colors. If done correctly, children will have a surprise picture when finished.

SURPRISE SQUARES !

Color in ORANGE all the squares that say *fast*.

Color in BROWN all the squares that say *some*.

Color in GREEN all the squares that say *was*.

When you are done you will have a surprise picture.

was	was	was	was	was	saw	won	son	sing	warm	us
was	was	was	was	saw	wall	sow	soon	same	sleep	find
some	some	saw	same	soon	saw	wall	soon	same	warm	find
some	same	has	wish	fire	saw	soon	some	some	first	first
some	sum	first	wish	first	saw	soon	some	fast	fast	fat
some	sum	first	fast	fast	fast	fast	some	fast	fast	first
some	seem	first	fast	fist	soon	fast	some	some	far	saw
some	moon	first	fast	first	frost	fast	soon	same	far	saw
some	saw	saw	fast	five	wall	fast	first	saw	soon	saw
some	was	was	was	was	was	was	was	was	was	was

Title:	**"Mix and Match"**
Purpose:	To give children practice in visual discrimination.
Activity:	Group.
Materials:	Mimeographed sheet or blackboard and chalk.
Procedure:	Use sets of easily confused letters to make up the exercise. Say, "Some letters look somewhat alike. This lesson will help you tell them from one another. Put your pencil on the dot at the top of the page. Trace over the line with your pencil. This is the direction you must read words. Do the lesson in this direction. First look at the letters on the first line in column A. Trace them with your pencil. Two of the letters are missing in column B and three letters are missing in column C. Put them in and trace the letters that are done for you. In column D you must put in all the letters. Put them in the same order they are in Column A. Check to see if your letters in column D match those in column A. Then proceed to line 2."

	A	B	C	D
1.	n h n n	n - - n	- - - n	- - - -
2.	s z v o	- z v -	- z - -	- - - -
3.	b d p q	b - - q	- d - -	- - - -
4.	r n h r	r - - r	- - h -	- - - -
5.	v w r x	- - r x	- w - -	- - - -
6.	l t i j	- t - j	- t - -	- - - -
7.	a c e o	a - e -	- c - -	- - - -

Title:	**"Find It, Take It"**
Purpose:	To develop student's visual discrimination skills.
Activity:	Group.
Materials:	Two sets of word cards.
Procedure:	Make word cards, two of each. Put the cards with tape on their backs on the board. Select two teams. Call out a word. The first person in each team to run up and pick out the word you have said gets a point for his team. The words should be mixed up for each item.

Illustration:

man	bug	sun	ten	cat	jug	bus	cup
six	tub	box	rat	man	hen	log	pen
bid	leg	pig	map	cot	map	tub	fan
nut	ban	cup	jug	six	rat	gun	pig
hen	fan	rug	dog	dog	ten	leg	bus
hat	fan	rug	dog	bed	bag	rug	box
bag	bus	gun	cot	pin	bat	ban	lip
bat	lip	log	cat	nut	hen	cap	sun

Title:	**"Flannelboard Matching"**
Purpose:	To develop visual discrimination.
Activity:	Group (4-6).
Procedure:	Take a flannelboard and about ten to 12 pictures with names on separate pieces of papers. I would have them spread out so that the children could see all of them at once. Then, I would hold up a picture and ask a child what the picture described, and ask him to locate the word which described the picture. Once he found the matching pair, he would be allowed to put them on the flannelboard. To small children, this is a real honor! If a child misses a picture-word combination, it would be passed on to the next in line, to see if he can answer it correctly. If he can do so, he can put it on the flannelboard, but if he should miss, it goes on to the next person until someone can answer it correctly. If none can get the right answer, the teacher will explain to them what the word was, and she should go back to that word later on in the game.

The purpose of this game is to help the children learn picture recognition. It is also very helpful for visual discrimination. This also teaches them word recognition. When the children are just learning new words, this game is quite important for them. It is much easier to learn new words if they are written large, and thoroughly explained. This game also gives them reason for learning the words, and not just, "So that you can learn to read."

This game, as above stated, is won by the child who answers the greatest number of questions correctly. It could also be changed to two teams, and if one person misses a word the other team is given a chance to answer it. If the second team answers it correctly, they are given the point. After each correct answer, the "up" team changes. The team with the greatest number of points at the end of the designated time wins the game. The only thing wrong with the playing of this game as a team game is that it causes more competition amongst the children. This is not bad except that there is already so much of it maybe we should try not to cause anymore. Many people disagree on this point saying that they need the competion because they will be faced with it when they get out in the "cruel, hard" world. To this point I would say—a little bit of anything is good, but too much can be harmful!

FLANNELBOARD (finished product)

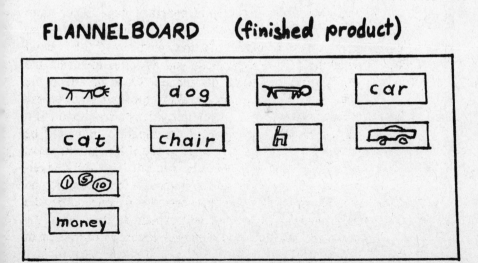

Title: **"Visual Discrimination"**

Purpose: To check visual discrimination ability.

Activity: Group or independent.

Materials: Ditto sheets and crayons of various colors.

Procedure: Make ditto work sheets on which there are four rows with three to four objects in a row. Row 1: four boys, three hold a baseball, one does not. Row 2: four ducks, three have tails and one does not. Row 3: four trees, three are palm trees, one is not. Row 4: four balls, three have stripes, one has dots. Give a sheet to each child making sure each child has crayons too. Explain to the children that there is one object in Row 1 that is different and that when they find it, they are to circle it with their red crayon. Do the same with rows 2, 3, and 4 using blue, yellow and black crayons.

You could also have another sheet with various shapes on it such as triangles, squares, circles, etc. in different sizes. Have the children circle which is different in each row with a different colored crayon each time. Example: Row 1—a large square, a small square, and a circle. Row 2—a small triangle, a small circle and a large triangle.

These tests will also show the teacher whether or not the child knows his colors.

AUDITORY DISCRIMINATION

Title: **"Rhyming Words"**

Purpose: To develop auditory and visual acuity.

Activity: Group.

Materials: Flannelboard, cards printed with rhyming words and some non-rhyming words. Teacher would have a set of cards (a different color) which would have a word to use for rhyming a particular ending.

Procedure: Pass out all cards to the group except teacher deck. Teacher puts a word on flannelboard and children having a rhyming word hold up their hands, then each places his card under the main word. This goes on until only the non-rhyming words are left. Group can be divided into teams.

Title: **"Picture Word Lotto"**

Purpose: To help students acquire auditor discrimination.

Activity: Game.

Procedure: Picture Word Lotto is designed to help the players gain skill in auditory discrimination by listening to the "caller" pronounce a word and understanding the spoken word. The player can also gain and strengthen concepts by the use of pictures which are to be matched with the appropriate representative word. The game is fun and serves as a motivating force. The game can result in a winning player if the teacher desires that there be a winner, and rewards can be offered to the winner also if desired by the teacher.

Each player receives a playing card (cards could be made from tagboard) which is similar to the card used in Bingo. Words are used instead of numbers. Each player also has collection of small pictures which correspond to the words printed on the card. The entire class can play the game but in order to avoid confusion, smaller groups of about ten players should be used. The teacher should allow the students who are having difficulty in auditory discrimination have many opportunities to play the game. One "caller" is needed to pronounce the words. This would be the teacher or one of the students.

The "caller" pronounces a word which is the same as a word on the players' cards. Not all of the players' cards will have the same words, but each player is given pictures which represent all of the possible words. The player must select from his collection of pictures the picture which corresponds to the word. He then tries to match the picture with the printed word if it appears on his card. A player can be the winner when he has pictures arranged in a line across the card or on the diagonal.

Title:	**"Fun with Speech"**
Purpose:	Drill to distinguish phonetic elements.
Activity:	Group or individual.
Materials:	List of words with the sound you wish to work on.
Procedure:	Have the children get in a large circle and stoop down. The teacher will tell them which letter sound to listen for. Now, tell them if they hear the "l" sound to jump up, Say the word "lollypop," For those who do not jump up, repeat the word and stress the "l". Try more words until you feel that they are hearing the sound quite well. Then use different letter sounds.
	Variation: Arrange 3 chairs in a row. The first is the beginning sound, the second is the middle sound and the third is the ending sound. Say a word and ask a child to sit in the correct chair. Example: *s*oup (for S)—The child sits in the first chair. For the word bu*s* he would sit in the third chair.

Title:	**"Rhyme Time"**
Purpose:	To provide practice in auditory perception.
Activity:	Individual or small group.
Materials:	A number of 3 x 4 inch picture rhyming cards, example: bed and sled.

Procedure: The picture cards are placed along the chalk tray. The first child goes to the board and picks up the first card and says the name of the object. He then moves along the chalk tray until he finds a picture card rhyming with his first card. He keeps both cards if he says correctly the name of each picture.

Alternative Procedure: 1. As individual child may play the game by laying rhyming cards, side by side on the table.

2. To add an element of difficulty, more than two rhyming words for the same sound may be included.

Title: **"Sounds All Around"**

Purpose: To provide *listening* training,

Activity: Group.

Procedure: Ask students to sit very still with their eyes closed for a full minute and *listen*. Then list any sound heard on the chalkboard. Again with their eyes closed, the teacher makes a deliberate sound. The student who correctly identifies the sound then gets to make the next sound.

ALPHABET SEQUENCE AND IDENTIFICATION

Title: **"Alphabet Sequence Board"**

Purpose: To provide further practice with the sequence of the alphabet.

Activity: Small groups or individual.

Materials: Alphabet sequence board (can be a piece of posterboard). Glue on five rows of pockets. Make each pocket row about 1¼ inches wide. The pocket rows are then divided into 26 smaller pockets by numbering the pockets from 1 to 26. There are 26 cards with pictures of objects pasted on them to represent each letter of the alphabet. There is another set of 26 smaller cards with the letters of the alphabet written on them.

Procedure: The student uses the alphabet sequence board to place the letters of the alphabet in alphabetical order. They also place pictures of objects in alphabetical order according to the first letter of that object.

The first step for the children is to place the pictures representing the letters of the alphabet in proper sequence. They then use the smaller cards with the letters of the alphabet and place them in the pockets with the picture. Later, they may use the letters of the alphabet alone. The picture and letter cards should be placed in an envelope which is pasted on the back of the board. There should also be a key provided for this activity in order that the student may check his own work.

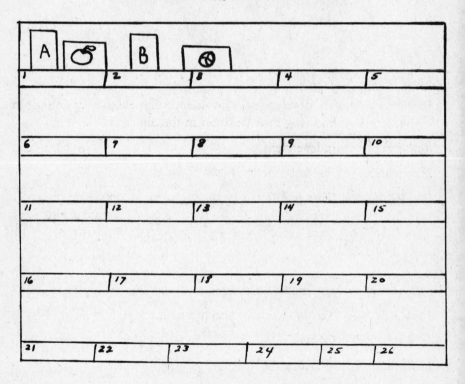

Title: **"Alphabet Letters"**

Purpose: To recognize alphabet letters.

Activity.   Game.

Materials: Six large pages with four or five letters of the alphabet on each page.
Six sets of objects for childrren.

Procedure: Begin, ''We have been studying the alphabet and now I have a game to see what you remember.''

Do one page a day, or for several days, depending on the children. Ask the boys and girls to name the alphabet letters as you point to them.

When a child names all the letters on a page, he receives a construction paper duplicate of the object. For instance, if the alphabet letters are on leaves, the child will receive a leaf to be pinned on his or her shirt.

The object is to know all the alphabet letters and thus get all the items.

Title: **''ABC File Box''**

Purpose: To develop skill in identifying beginning letters and knowing their position in the alphabet.

Activity: Independent.

Materials: File box. Index cards.

Procedure: Give pupils file boxes with cards containing pictures of objects such as lamp and the word. Let them alphabetize them according to the first letter in each word.

Title: **''Alphabetize Game''**

Purpose: To give students practice in learning how to alphabetize.

Activity: Game.

Materials: Word cards.

Procedure: Make out a list of words on cards. Mix them up on the chalkboard. Pick two teams. Have at least five cards for each team. After cards have been placed, have the first person on each team place the cards in alphabetical order. The first person to alphabetize them correctly gets one point for his team.

BEFORE

| lay | sit | you | could | play |

AFTER

| could | lay | play | sit | you |

Title:	**"Alphabet Capitals"**
Purpose:	To develop alphabetical sequence.
Activity:	Game.
Materials:	3½" squares with capital letters, set of cards (26 capitals).
Procedure:	Divide class in half. Say, "Today we are going to play a game with the alphabet. I want one person from Team One to find the first letter of the alphabet. Team Two locates the next letter, etc. If a team misses, the other team gets two turns. The team with the most letters is the winner. Letters can be mixed.

CHALKBOARD

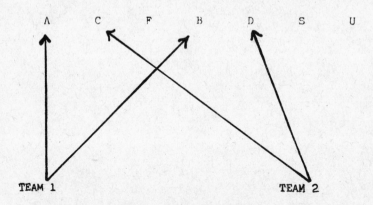

The teacher asks Team 1 to find letters A, B, and F.
The team gets only two letters so that Team 2 can
have two turns, and so on.

Title: **"Recognizing the Alphabet"**

Purpose: To recognize the sequence of the alphabet and word families.

Activity: Group or independent.

Materials: Two worksheets.

Procedure: Worksheet One (with an apple): Students connect the letters to form the apple. The students match the words at the bottom of the page.

Worksheet Two: Students find and circle the word that matches the first word.

WORKSHEET ONE

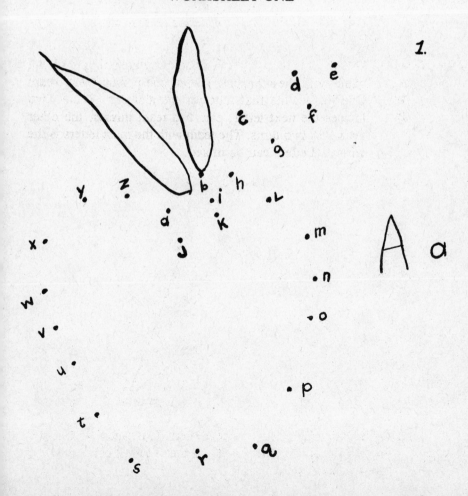

MATCH:

	a	b		a	b
	an	man		ant	pant
	can	pan		and	hands
	man	fan		Ann	ant
	tan	can		pant	hand
	fan	an		hand	and
	pan	tan		hands	Ann

WORKSHEET TWO

Circle:

an	can	tan	an	fan
tan	fan	can	man	tan
fan	tan	fan	can	man
man	man	tan	fan	can
can	an	man	can	tan
ant	pant	and	hand	**ant**
and	ant	and	pant	hand
pant	and	hand	**ant**	pant
hand	man	and	hand	an

Title:	**"Dominoes"**
Purpose.	To develop skill in alphabet recognition.
Activity:	Small groups.
Materials:	Cover matchboxes with paper and write or draw letters and pictures on each card.

Procedure: Match ends of dominoes by matching letters or matching beginning letters and picture symbols.

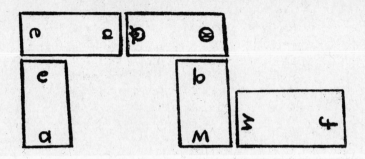

Title: **"Word Bingo"**

Purpose: To improve the child's ability to recognize the sounds of letters and letter blends.

Activity: Game.

Materials: Enough bingo cards with word letters and blends for each student, and small squares to cover the squares containing the right letter.

Procedure: Each student should have a card with letters and blends in each square, and the game should be played like bingo. When the instructor says a word, the students who have the letter the word begins with on their card should cover it with a square until one child has four in a row——horizontally, vertically, or diagonally.

D	R	S	St
P	Sh	K	C
A	M	T	B
F	Tr	L	N

Word called:

street

Title:	**"Recognizing Letters"**
Purpose:	To develop alphabet letter recognition.
Activity:	Individual or group.
Materials:	Magazines, paste, scissors, crayons, newsprint.
Procedure:	Children are given pictures of advertisements from magazines with large lettering to locate and cut out words containing a given letter. They then paste or tape the words onto a piece of newsprint and circle with crayon the letter or letters they were to locate.
Illustration:	The teacher gives the children advertisements from magazines that contain several of the letter "e". The children will (1) locate and cut out words containing the letter "e"; (2) paste the words on the newsprint; (3) circle with crayon all of the e's that appear in their words.

Title:	**"Flash Cards"**
Purpose:	To associate pictures of objects with written words, initial sounds, and initial letters.
Activity:	Group or independent.
Materials:	Magazines, scissors, paste, 5″ x 8″ index cards, crayons or magic markers, shoe-caddy bags.
Procedure:	After introducing a letter and the sound it makes at the beginning of a word, children will be given magazines to locate and cut out pictures of objects having the same beginning sound as the letter they are studying. The children paste their pictures on the 5″ x 8″ index cards. The children then place their cards in their own pockets on the shoe caddy, which is to them a "card caddy." The teacher checks the pictures to see that the children correctly matched the picture with the sound, and, depending on the ability of the child, will write the word of the picture on the back of the card and underline the initial sound or letter or have the child do this. The children will continue doing this until they have a complete set of "flash cards." The flash cards may also be expanded to

include diphthongs, vowel sounds, silent letters, prefixes, tenses, etc., depending on the age of the children and their abilities.

Illustration: One child may locate a picture of a tomato to illustrate the beginning sound of the letter "t." He would cut out the tomato and paste it on a 5″ x 8″ index card and mark a "t" on the back with a magic marker or crayon. He would then put his card in his pocket of the "card caddy" for the teacher to check later. Since the tomato picture is an illustration of the initial sound of "t," she would write "tomato" on the back of the card and underline the "t." The child would use the card to test himself or his friends, first by naming the letter which tomato "starts with" and later, by turning the card over and matching the word and letter with the picture—tomato.

CARD CADDY		
DON	SALLY	JIM
PAT	ROBIN	LYNN
JACK	LEE	FAYE

Title: **"Alphabet Book"**

Purpose: To familiarize the children with the letters of the alphabet.

Activity: Group.

Materials: Illustration board, felt and felt tip pens in various colors, yarn, glue, and scissors. Make an alphabet book of felt letters. Beside each letter on a page, is a picture of an object (beginning with that letter) which is familiar to the child. Print the name of the object above the picture, emphasizing the first letter. The soft letters should encourage the children to touch and trace over them.

Procedure: The teacher should first introduce the book to the class, using questions similar to these—What letter do you see? What word do you think is written above the picture? The class should be encouraged to bring in pictures of objects that begin with the letter, the next day. To start with, only one or two letters should be introduced and those previously studied should be reviewed. Later, the book can be placed in an area where children can use it to practice.

Illustration: The Alphabet Book has soft, felt letters, pictures of the familiar objects beginning with the letters, and the names of the objects—with the beginning letter emphasized.

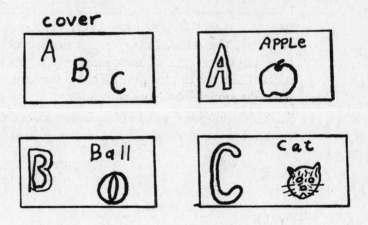

Title: **"Alphabet Rhythm"**

Purpose: To acquaint children with the letters of the alphabet.

Activity: Game.

Procedure: Have pupils sit in a circle on the floor. They should hit hands on their knees twice, clap their hands twice, snap their fingers first on the right hand and then the left. This should be done to a definite rhythm pattern—1-2-3-4-5-6. The first child says the letter "A" as he snaps his right hand and then a word beginning with the letter as he snaps his left hand. Children keep the rhythm pattern as they continue around the circle. If a child misses the rhythm, or fails to call a letter or word, then he is out of the game.

Illustration: Slap-—Slap—Clap—Clap—A—apple.

UNDERSTANDING STORY SEQUENCE

Title: **"The Comic Strip Puzzle"**

Purpose: To provide practice in development of sequence.

Activity: Game.

Procedure: Cut apart the comic strips from an old newspaper. Shuffle and put the parts of each comic strip in a labeled envelope. The children are given envelopes with instructions to put the parts of the comic strip in proper story order. Once the children are finished, they either tell or write the stories they have put together.

         For older children, one can place a part from a different comic strip into each envelope to increase the difficulty.

Title: **"What Am I?"**

Purpose: To help children with visual perception and practice in following a sequence of numbers.

Activity: Group.

Materials: Duplicated sheets.

Procedure: The teacher distributes duplicated sheets, one to each student and asks them to locate number 1. She then asks them what comes after 1 and they draw a line to 2. They continue following the numbers in chronological order until their picture is completed and they can identify the picture.

WHAT AM I ?

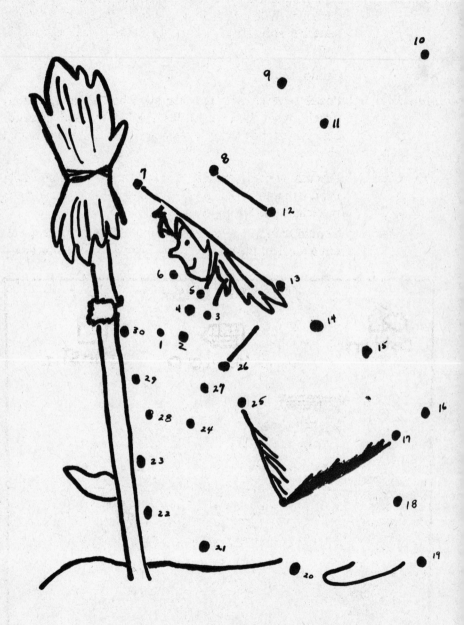

I AM A _____

Title: **"Sense Perception"**

Purpose: To have students feel texture of materials and associate the touch with words which describe the texture of the material; soft, firm, smooth, and rough (concept building).

Activity: Group.

Materials: Poster covered with red felt; swatches of satin, cotton, plastic, wool, felt, velvet, leather, burlap, lace, and rubber. Small box with swatches of material mentioned above.

Procedure: Discuss word "material," and "texture." Also, soft, firm, smooth, and rough. Go over poster naming the material with the children.

Let children put hand in box and with eyes closed, pull out a piece of material. Child may feel materials on board

and with the piece of material he pulled from the box behind his back, he will match it to the correct one on the board. He will then state whether it is smooth, rough, firm, or soft. Or he may use other words to describe it. Also, he could put words on board to classify materials.

Put poster and box at a table where children may feel the material and try to match the materials by themselves or with a partner.

Subject Skill Index

Subject Skill Index

HANDWRITING

Cursive

Cursive Introduction, 83
Cursive Writing Championship, 90
Copying Poems, 95
Finish Writing, 84
Frame It, 83
Letter C, 86
Letter O, 85
Mouse Mystery, 93

General Activities for both Cursive and Manuscript

Handwriting Technicalities, 86
I Am, 89
Making Calendars, 82
My Scratch Box, 81
Poetry and Handwriting, 92
Relaxing Handwriting, 92
Riddles, 88
Self-Description, 91
Using Clichés for Alignment Practice, 93

Manuscript

Alphabet Fish, 90
Crayon Pictures, 96
Find the Secret Message, 80
Finish Writing, 84
Skill Sheets, 81

LANGUAGE READINESS

Alphabet Sequence and Identification

ABC File Box, 245
Alphabet Book, 251
Alphabet Capitals, 246
Alphabetize Game, 245
Alphabet Letters, 244
Alphabet Rhythm, 252
Alphabet Sequence Board, 243
Dominoes, 248
Flash Cards, 250
Recognizing Letters, 250
Recognizing the Alphabet, 247
Word Bingo, 249

Auditory Discrimination

Fun with Speech, 242
Picture Word Lotto, 241
Rhyme Time, 242
Rhyming Words, 241
Sounds All Around, 243

Oral Language (See Oral Communication)

Understanding Story Sequence

The Comic Strip Puzzle, 253
What Am I?, 253

Visual Discrimination

Find It, Take It, 238
Flannelboard Matching, 238
Mix and Match, 237
Surprise Squares!, 236
Visual Discrimination, 240

ORAL COMMUNICATION

General Oral Language Development

Describing Characters, 75
Descript-O, 55
Dial-A-Topic, 62
Goofies, 66
Informal Talking, 75
Introduce Me, 63
Mirror, Mirror . . . , 56
Open-ended Questions, 65
Opinions Please, 73
Speak and Listen to One Another, 62
Talking People, 76
Telephone Communication, 63
Telephoning, 63
Use of Telephone, 72
What Do You See?, 55

Listening Skill Development

Can You Guess the Sound?, 57
Fact or Opinion, 60
From Here to There, 60
Listening Detectives, 58
Listening Relay, 54
Look, Listen, Learn, 59
Magic Picture, 58
Mysterious Object, 57
Practice Making Introductions, 74
Shake A Sound, 59
Word Back, 54

Speaking Skill Development

Advertising Specials, 72
Choral Reading, 67
Combating Stage Fright, 65
Five Little Pumpkins Sitting on a Gate, 70
Freeze, 73
Interviewing and Reporting, 56
Morning News Report, 68
Picture Stimulus, 69
Poetry, 71
Projecting to Inanimate Objects, 68